Prospering WOMAN

A COMPLETE GUIDE

TO ACHIEVING THE

FULL, ABUNDANT LIFE

RUTH ROSS, PH.D.

NEW WORLD LIBRARY
NOVATO, CALIFORNIA

New World Library
14 Pamaron Way
Novato, CA 94949

Cover photography: Shelley Firth
Editorial: Gina Misiroglu
Typography: Stephanie Eichleay
Printed by: Malloy Lithographing, Inc.

Library of Congress Cataloging-in-Publication Data

Ross, Ruth, 1929–1994
Prospering woman : a complete guide to
achieving the full, abundant life / Ruth Ross. — Rev. ed.
p.   cm.
ISBN 1-880032-60-0 (acid-free paper)
1. Women — Life skills guides.   2. Women — Psychology.
3. Success.   4. Sex role.   I. Title.
HQ1221.R72   1995
305.42 — dc20   94-38598 CIP

Revised Edition — First Printing, May 1995
Printed in the U.S.A.
Distributed by Publishers Group West
10 9 8 7 6 5 4 3 2

Prospering WOMAN

CONTENTS

PUBLISHER'S PREFACE
TO THE SECOND EDITION

When the first edition of *Prospering Woman* was published, we were still a young company, struggling with many of the problems of small start-up businesses, just beginning to have some glimmerings of possible prosperity after having published *Creative Visualization*, our first truly successful title.

One day a manuscript arrived in the mail with a cover letter from a woman named Ruth Ross. She thanked us for publishing *Creative Visualization*, and told us that we should publish her manuscript next, for they were related titles in many important ways.

After just a few minutes with the manuscript, I realized she was right. *Prospering Woman* is an inspiring and empowering book; one that we were proud to publish. The book first came out in 1982, and became one of the best-selling books our company has ever published.

Although written primarily for women, the book has proven very effective and useful for me and a lot of other men as well. Trusting our intuition and focusing on our other qualities of compassion, cooperation, insight, and imagination can help all of us — male and female — build the future of our dreams.

Shortly after publishing the book, we started receiving all kinds of mail from readers. Here is one of my favorites:

> "I want to thank you for writing *Prospering Woman*. I am over-joyed by the book. It gives the woman who lacks self-confidence the tools to pick herself up and become a capable, confident woman."

Here it is in a brand-new edition that Ruth's daughters, Kathy Hartwig and Becky Davis, gave us. It was fully updated by Ruth Ross, just before she passed on, to continue growing and being successful and inspiring others, I'm sure, in some far greater way.

Marc Allen
May 1995

PREFACE

WHY A BOOK ON PROSPERITY FOR WOMEN?

*T*he purpose of *Prospering Woman* is to show you how natural it is to prosper. Prosperity is experiencing balance in life; it is attaining what we want on mental, physical, emotional, spiritual *and* financial levels. Prosperity is a natural result of opening our minds to our creative imaginations and being willing to act on our ideas. From this perspective, to prosper is a human right, having nothing to do with being either female or male.

Nevertheless, many of us have negative feelings about what it means for *women* to prosper. Why is it that the closer many women come to personal success, the more uncomfortable we become inside? Part of the answer seems to lie in how we have, until now, defined prosperity and success, and part is in the fact that as women, we are programmed and have programmed ourselves not to prosper.

Women have associated being successful in the world with being male for so long that, as we cross an invisible role line and learn to become stronger, more independent, and successful in our own right, we may feel a tightening in our gut. This feeling tells us we're getting close to the perimeters of an earlier programming. We feel the effects of our unspoken, unwritten agreement that to personally prosper is to be unfeminine.

The key to getting out of this programming is to take a new look at what true prosperity is. In the past, prosperity has been almost totally defined in traditional, aggressive, competitive male terms. It required behavior "unbecoming" to women who have been expected to exert only their softness and have been applauded mainly for serving and supporting others. The emerging woman finds herself in conflict with these terms or assumed values.

The stereotyped male success pattern does not fit our needs. Our journey is neither to dress up like men — or imitate men in any way — or to compete like men, using their definitions. We need a new perspective, a "paradigm shift" in redefining what true prosperity and success are.

From this new perspective, prosperity is clearly not role- or gender-determined. It is the result of having developed a "consciousness of prosperity" — realizing that as human beings we have all the tools we need to create our prosperity. It is being fulfilled in the highest sense — experiencing peace of mind as well as having an abundance of wealth, health, and happiness in life.

It is time for both women and men to be powerful and successful — not because of their sex, but because they are human. Women and men alike will appreciate and use the tools found in this book, for the principles of prosperity are the same for all. You men will not only learn new ways to create abundance for yourselves and find support for your efforts to create a success in broader, more humanistic terms, you will also understand more about the prospering women in your lives, and how to assist those you want to see prosper.

Women will learn how to "deprogram" their sex role training and allow themselves to prosper, and feel good about it. The "holistic approach" to abundance does not require that women deny their feminine natures. The opposite is true. *Prospering Woman* is proposing a shift in perspective — a new look at how feminine values and characteristics lend themselves to the prospering process.

For example, women have always known, intuitively, the importance of balance in designing a successful life. Many of us have watched high-achieving men reach the top financially only to find their empires crumble because their success was not balanced. This imbalance might be evident in a broken home, a wife divorcing from lack of real contact, children drifting without sincere care and guidance, friends gone from lack of depth in relationships, or health broken from too little personal attention and self-love.

Many women, viewing this picture from the sidelines, have concluded that money acquired without the balance of a satisfying, loving life is an empty gain. Many of them have simply opted out, or decided to gain their "wealth" through dependency, not independence.

This is not the time for women to retreat into dependency. This is, instead, the time for women to assert their own values and beliefs and to affirm their personal power.

World problems cry out today for all of us to help in formulating new values and perceiving new answers. The very characteristics that women have been acknowledged for, and that many men are beginning to appreciate in themselves as well — intuitive awareness, vivid imaginative processes, empathy, sensitivity, and nurturing — are all needed in order to succeed and prosper at every level of life.

These attributes are an integral part of our human nature, and an important aspect of achieving true prosperity in the world in ways heretofore undreamed of. By finally acknowledging the power of the intuitive, imaginative side of ourselves, we have access to our enlightened imagination, and to the full creative power of our minds. These are the basic tools for our prosperity.

Women have been raised to be dependent thinkers,
not prosperity thinkers. This book is dedicated
to the thousands of women out there
who are daily changing their thinking
and changing their lives.

WHAT IS PROSPERITY?

All prosperity begins in the mind and is dependent only
upon the full use of our creative imagination.

Have you ever had a "magic day" when everything worked? On those days, you enjoyed the fruits of your actions without straining to achieve — you got what you went after seemingly without effort. Simply put, you accomplished what you set out to do — no matter what it was.

Magic days and a feeling of prosperity go hand in hand. When we feel prosperous our days seem magical. We live life from a center of contentment. We experience an inner knowingness that all is well — that we have a place in the world and that somehow we know we are in the right place at the right time. This sense of peace and contentment with oneself is what I call "true prosperity," and requires a shift in consciousness to maintain.

Beyond that, living prosperously involves having the power to create a life of your choice — to get what you really want, not just what you're handed. You first need to become aware of your power of prosperity before you can deliberately bring it under your conscious control and create a life of abundance. This book is about how to be in touch with your power to make that shift in consciousness and thus make your life a succession of magic days.

Although no two magic days are alike, sometimes hearing another's story can help us remember our own. Here is the first of several prosperity profiles I hope will remind you of times when you, too, have tuned into your prospering energy and made "unbelievable" things happen.

PROSPERITY PROFILE NO. 1
Mary Ann's Story

Mary Ann Shaffer sat in the living room of her small suburban home in Los Angeles, feeling her usual vague sense of discontentment. She wanted something more in life — but she wasn't sure what it was. She watched the hands of the clock. The children were in school until three; with his new job, her husband would not be home for another week. Why had she agreed to move here anyway? She knew no one in this entire city, she had no special plans of her own, and there was nothing she was particularly excited about doing.

Everything seemed to close in on her that day — almost forcing a change. The weather had been bad all week — hot and muggy. The house had felt intolerably small. She wanted to get out, do something — but what? And where?

The negative thought patterns that usually led to resignation came up for her again. She considered a job, but knew she wanted to be home with the children while they were still young. What could she do anyway? Her interests were reading and writing, her work skills limited and rusty from being home for four years. This morning, however, these thoughts weren't enough to appease her restlessness.

The "magic" feeling started when she decided she *had* to do something — it was time. Her actions that followed from that moment made no particular sense to her, but somehow she felt she had to follow through on her inner yearning.

In the past few weeks she had frequently allowed herself to day-dream about what she really wanted. This morning it paid off. She remembered that in college she had always wanted to write. She couldn't ignore any longer that she still wanted to.

A sheet of white paper lay on the desk in front of her. She felt as if she were making a statement to the world when she declared in big, bold letters: I WANT TO WRITE. Thinking a minute longer, she added: I want a job writing. She remembered she didn't have a good typewriter, and thought as long as she was doing this, she might as well go all out. She wrote: I want a new typewriter — for free.

Suddenly she got up and stretched. This felt better. "Why not ask for what I want? — I deserve it!" What did she want to write about? Books, of course — her other love! At the bottom of the page she wrote: I want to write about books — good books. She folded the paper and put it in the desk drawer.

With a rush of energy, she picked up her purse and walked out the door. As she told the story later, she recalled an uncanny feeling at that moment — a feeling as if she were full of purpose.

By five o'clock that evening, Mary Ann had a job writing for several newspapers. Her specific writing assignment was to critique the latest books coming out in the fields she was interested in. And she was the proud owner of a brand new typewriter that didn't cost her a cent. That job later developed into writing a popular column which lasted several years, and led to a whole new career working in creative writing. What had happened that day?

Although she didn't know it, Mary Ann had tuned into a *prosperity flow* — a creative energy that we all have available to us at all times. Unconsciously, she had used the laws of prosperity to bring about dynamic positive change in her life. Like most of us caught in the excitement of that flow, she didn't understand her feelings at the time.

Walking down the street she had felt puzzled. How could she feel so resolved when she had nowhere to go? She had no answer for the nagging, scolding voice inside, which demanded to know what she was doing and where she was going. Was she planning to walk up and down the street until she found a job? She ignored the voice, but she did feel foolish. Another part of her was in charge now, and she couldn't rationalize or justify it. "Why not act like a fool?" she thought. "Being reasonable hasn't always helped me."

When she impulsively entered her favorite local bookstore, she was greeted by Sid, the owner, asking her if she had read the new Harold Robbins book. She answered, "Yes, wasn't it awful?" That remark started a conversation quite unlike any other she had had with this usually reserved man. After fifteen minutes or so of laughing and telling each other their favorite book stories, another customer, who had obviously eavesdropped, approached them. He gave Mary Ann his card, and asked if she had ever reviewed books. She said no, but he continued to hold out his card. He said he was the editor of several local newspapers and could use someone with her enthusiasm and insight into writing — if she was interested.

Seeing the look on Mary Ann's face, the bookstore owner, caught up in the excitement of the moment, offered Mary Ann full use of all the current books to critique if she took the job. She thanked them both, made an appointment for an interview the next day, and jubilantly walked out of the store on air.

"Now," she told herself, "go for the typewriter." When she took her old typewriter into the appliance shop and was offered only $20.00 for it, her heart sank. The new ones were $120.00 and her budget couldn't be stretched. She had no way of knowing the other woman waiting to be helped would "just happen" to say loudly, "If I only had a few more Green Stamps, I could get this TV set for free." Mary Ann "just happened" to have a box full of Green Stamps in her car — two years' worth. She hated to paste them in, but didn't want to throw them away. She couldn't believe her ears when the woman offered her $80.00 for them.

The store owner, who had followed the two of them out to the car, stood fascinated. "Look lady, with this $80.00, and the $20.00

from your old typewriter — well, I was gonna mark those Olympics down to $100.00 in two months anyway. Why don't you take one of those home with you, and I'll mark down the price now?"

Something special had happened that day. Mary Ann didn't have a name for it, but she knew it was special. It wasn't just the job and the typewriter — it was something beyond that. She knew she had been witness to something she had helped to create. She had done her part all right, but it was bigger than her efforts alone. She felt her whole physical being had changed — lightened. Her heart sang. Whatever it was, she knew she wanted more of it.

With the help of this book, you, too, will learn how to have more of "it." You will see how natural it is for you to prosper — to get what you want — what is truly fulfilling in your life. We are naturally creative beings with far more power to bring positive change into our lives than we've ever imagined. Becoming prosperous is the result of using the full potential of our minds, the attitude we take about ourselves and our relations with others. It's about how we approach life.

REDEFINING PROSPERITY

What is "prosperity"?

The old, commonly used definition means acquiring as much wealth and power as possible. As I am defining it, living prosperously doesn't mean being able to accumulate more toys, or harness the ability to manipulate others. It does mean experiencing a balanced, fulfilled life on all levels — mental, physical, emotional, spiritual, and financial. Unless we have all the platters spinning, we're without balance in our lives, and more feels empty rather than full.

Prosperity is a result of opening our minds to our creative imagination and being willing to act on our ideas for the good of all concerned. From this perspective, to prosper is a human right, having nothing to do with gender.

WHY A BOOK ON THE PROSPERING WOMAN?

For the last ten thousand years most of the civilized world has bought the masculine myth that human beings, as the highest species on earth, were the end product of evolution. As such, we are exempt, so the story goes, from the laws that have kept the balance in nature for millions of years.

According to this myth, man was divinely determined to conquer and rule nature. To many it seemed self-evident that nature's resources belonged to man to exploit as he saw fit, and few questioned that we were essentially under a manifesto to bring law and order to a wild and therefore useless world.

Is it any wonder that, until now, we have defined prosperity and success in aggressive, competitive masculine terms? We were not only at war against nature — extracting the best and leaving the rest — but we were at war with ourselves.

"Success" required behavior unbecoming to half the species — to women — the "softer sex" who were expected to assert themselves only in their respect and support for their men and their offspring.

The emerging woman finds herself in conflict with these exclusive roles and with this one-sided belief system. The feminine force (in both male and female) has always known, intuitively, the importance of balance in designing a successful life.

Confined in her actions to the personal side of life in much of her history, women have observed many "high achievers" reach the top financially only to find their empires crumble because their success was not balanced. This imbalance might be evident in a broken home; divorce from lack of real contact; children drifting without sincere care and guidance; friends gone from lack of depth in relationship; or health broken from too little personal attention and self-love.

Viewing this picture from the sidelines, many women concluded that money and success acquired without the balance of a satisfying love life is an empty gain. Many opted out, or decided to gain their wealth through dependency, not independence. Others waded in to do battle declaring, "I can do anything you can do better." Either way it has felt too often like a losing battle.

The world is changing. Many women and men are beginning to realize that, as a culture, we can no longer pay the price of excluding women from power and responsibility. Nature, too, is showing us we can no longer ignore her natural laws.

National and world problems demand that the very best in all of us be called forth to help in formulating new values and perceiving new answers. Time is short and our very planet is continuing to ail from the abuses of our past.

We women must learn to take our power back — to learn how to allow ourselves to prosper. Even though we may have been programmed to be dependent thinkers rather than prosperity thinkers, true prosperity does not require us to deny our feminine natures. The opposite is true. *Prospering Woman* is proposing a shift in perspective — a new look at how feminine values and characteristics lend themselves, in fact are crucial to, the prospering process in the largest sense. The time is past due to honor and follow the feminine spirit of intuitive power.

PROSPERITY POWER AND INTUITION

All prosperity begins in the mind and is dependent only upon the full use of our creative imagination. Thought is energy, and thought energy has the power to manifest. Manifestation means to produce, to cause to happen, to bring forth from the world of ideas to the physical world of reality.

Our minds have the power to create. This power comes from our ability to picture. Everything ever created by humans was first an imaginative idea in someone's mind. We are totally surrounded by these creative ideas manifested physically — from the cup of coffee in the morning to the TV program at night.

So prosperity is a product of the creative mind. Essentially it is a state of consciousness, an attitude. Having the consciousness of prosperity is knowing that you have the ability to live a wondrous life through the full use of your creative imagination. When you are totally open to your flow of creative ideas, and are willing to act on those that prosper all concerned, you are on your path to an abundant life.

The prosperity process involves recognizing that the world we live in is only an external form of whatever we are imagining inwardly. We create the world around us as we imagine it to be. We achieve and maintain the degree of well-being in the external world that we conceive ourselves having internally.

The image we carry is a reflection of our belief system. What we believe is what we achieve — nothing more, nothing less. The secret to success is to use the same imaginative process and belief system we've been using, unconsciously and haphazardly, to bring the positive changes we desire into our lives.

Prosperity cannot be forced with sheer willpower. It must be coaxed with imagination. Willpower may bring momentary superficial gain, but in any contest between will and imagination, imagination always wins as the stronger force.

Once we understand the power of imagination, we understand why prosperity must exist in our consciousness before it can manifest in our lives.

In practical terms, this means that before you can become prosperous, you must create an image in your mind of being prosperous.

WHAT IS A PROSPERING WOMAN?

While no one image or concept fits every prospering woman, she is generally one who not only wants a full life, but also has the self-awareness to know specifically what a full life is for her. She comes to know who she is as a person, and chooses a work medium that allows her to express herself well. She no longer needs to wait for freedom or approval, for she has found that her independence lies within her own self-acceptance.

Prosperity comes easily to her when she finds the secret of the ages: her security does not exist in any bank account, but in the full use of her creative ideas. For this reason, she has learned to tap the powers of her imagination, and put her thoughts into creative action. She is then able to create more choices that come with financial prosperity.

The prospering woman knows that to live in a prosperous condition is to feel free to do, be, and have more of what she truly wants. The feeling of prosperity, however, does not necessarily come with any certain amount of money.

Many top executives making $500,000 or more annually do not feel prosperous, but insecure and worried about a multiplicity of problems. Job security is not what it used to be. It is obvious, then, that any effective plan to achieve successful, material prosperity must also include consideration of what makes us feel prosperous.

What makes you feel prosperous?

One woman I know goes without lunch and instead buys flowers for herself — and feels full all day. Another prefers books to flowers. Another feels coddled when she can go out to lunch spontaneously without anything special to celebrate. It's important to know what makes you feel special, for feeling prosperous is a way of being in the world. It is a statement about how you see yourself and your relationship with others.

BARRIERS TO PROSPERITY

The attitudes you hold about yourself and others make up the most fundamental obstacle keeping you from your prosperity.

You deserve and can have what you desire in life, but just dabbling in occasional positive thinking won't do it. Our most powerful conceptual prospering patterns are operating at the unconscious level.

We have set in our minds the scope and limits of our own prosperity, based on long-held concepts and decisions about ourselves. These thoughts, though we are no longer conscious of them, constitute a preprogrammed agenda for ourselves in our subconscious mind. We will accomplish only that which we believe deep down is possible, according to our internal picture of ourselves. For this reason, all behavioral and mental change, to be long lasting and effective, must have the force of the imaginative mind behind it.

Prosperity, then, is an inside job — *it is a matter of transforming your consciousness.* You must find ways to let go of your old negative concepts of yourself as being inadequate, unsure, victimized, unworthy — whatever stands in the way of seeing yourself as a creator of plenty.

CONCENTRATED MIND ACTION

This book is about making unconscious processes conscious. "Concentrated mind action" is a term I use to define the natural mind process that we use to create our own world; a process of applying new techniques to the old ideas of the power of the mind. This is a step-by-step procedure to help you acknowledge and release blocks to prosperity, and fully utilize the powers of your mind to achieve your goals.

Humans are energy systems. We hold energy, dam it, refine it, direct it — with thought. By focusing thought, we channel the energy of the mind.

How you use this power of channeled energy will determine the quality of your life and the degree of your prosperity. Both are dependent upon the nature of your thought — positive and negative.

With concentrated mind action, you will learn to use your mind as a vehicle, a tool for your evolutionary growth. The highest purpose of the mind is to become ever more self-aware. In the process, as you deliberately choose to let go of negative thought patterns and create a space for events of a more positive nature to take place in your life, you will learn to use the power of your thoughts creatively and develop consciousness necessary to attain and sustain prosperity.

PROSPERITY CONSCIOUSNESS QUIZ

Only *thought* stands in our way of attaining what we want in life. We can have what we think we deserve, and what we believe we can have. Conversely, if we are convinced we shouldn't have or are unworthy of getting what we want, we will also unconsciously arrange to put whatever we need in our path to prevent our becoming successful.

How do you picture your prosperity? Use the following checklist as a guide for looking at your belief system about yourself. Answer as honestly as possible, and then become an unbiased observer. How do your answers indicate the ways you are promoting or preventing your prosperity?

The chapter numbers indicate where you can find information to help you develop your prosperity consciousness in each area.

Question	Chapter
Do I really want to succeed?	4
Can I remain a loving, giving person and still prosper?	2
Do I know myself and what I want?	10
Is it okay for me to prosper? Do I deserve it?	4
Have I defined my basic purpose in life?	2
Have I considered the price of becoming prosperous?	14
Am I willing to pay it?	14
Am I comfortable with the whole idea of money?	5
Do I feel at ease around wealthy people?	5
Can I see myself having what I want?	16
Am I afraid of succeeding?	4
Will my relations with men change if I'm prosperous?	4
What do I intend to do with my money?	5

There are no right or wrong answers, so don't judge yourself. We are all becoming the person we want to be. If we are overly judgmental about ourselves when we receive insights, the insights stop coming.

PROSPERITY PROFILES

Throughout the book you will find a series of prosperity profiles

— personal interviews with a variety of prospering women. Most qualify their situation as being in the process of becoming a prospering woman. No one is ever "there" or stays "there" all the time. Nevertheless, they have that consciousness of prosperity that allows them to feel fulfilled with a sense of who they are and what they want, and they are presently living out their dreams. My hope is that you can find yourself in these pages, and can benefit from their experience.

PROSPERING RESULTS

Everyone will benefit in different ways from the ideas expressed in this book. A young client of mine named Mary was able to use the prospering concepts to overcome seemingly desperate circumstances. At twenty-nine, she was deeply depressed. Her husband had died the year before. Her sense of loss was compounded by the fear of poverty looming endlessly before her. She had two small children to support, few marketable skills, and no recent work experience. Her health was declining as a result of her depression and lack of self-care.

Using the "concentrated mind action" process, she learned to relax, accept what had to be accepted — the finality of the death — and work with the possibilities that life offered. As she learned to let go of the old (memories in this case), she actually created space in her life for the new. She learned to take her mind off her negative image of herself and look at who she really was. With a new consciousness, she was able to acknowledge her strengths and weaknesses and recognize all the possibilities around her. With newfound confidence, she was able to take advantage of them, finally accepting a job which she had previously been fearful of accepting. Her health improved as her depression lifted, and she has since gone on to establish her own successful business in the same field.

As you develop a consciousness of prosperity, you will experience improvement in circumstances almost immediately. We are meant to be prosperous, but like everything else, the process is as important as the end result. At first, for example, when you learn to clear your mind and focus with intent, you can experience improved mental ability with greater concentration, recall of detail, or a heightened sensory awareness.

When you are learning to "picture" your own success, you may find yourself increasingly effective at current tasks. This will produce a more positive self-image and greater self-confidence.

Relationships improve. Learning to listen and respond to opposing inner wishes often reduces internal conflict and produces greater peace of mind. When you project a more positive inner attitude, conflict with others is reduced.

As your sensory awareness increases, you are more keenly alert to early warning signals of impending ill health. Good eating and exercise programs are more easily maintained using your mental energies in a positive way.

This book is the beginning of a new adventure. Choosing prosperity as a way of life means you are opening creative channels in ever-greater proportions. Financial reward is important, but true prosperity is finding a context within which you can best express your total self. You will continually see higher and bigger challenges as you increase awareness of your uniqueness and what you truly value. By using the prosperity keys and laws introduced throughout this book, you can replace old, limiting beliefs with a new, more healthy outlook on yourself and your life, producing prosperous conditions in all areas of your life.

Part One:

Releasing

T he purpose of Part One, Releasing, is to set the foundation for your new prosperity, allowing you to uncover concepts that are acting as barriers in your life. The keys to prosperity will help you release the habitual thought patterns that came as part of the package of the female role: low self-image and restrictive concepts of self in relation to money, power, love, and success.

As the Zen master illustrated in attempting to pour a cup of tea for his student when the cup was already full, becoming empty is also part of the process. If you are already filled with concepts that are not conducive to prosperity, you will not be in a position to allow new ideas to affect you. We must release to prepare to receive.

After completing this inner work, you will then be ready for Part Two, Receiving. In a step-by-step procedure, you will learn how to use the laws of prosperity in a concentrated mind action process. By combining concentrated thought and imagination, you will be able to reprogram that subconscious agenda of "making do" for newer, conscious goals of prosperity.

2

PROSPERITY AND PURPOSE

*Money, success, power, fame, prestige, and spirituality
are all interrelated — they are our inner and
outer work at one and the same time.*

Starting to learn *how* to prosper without first considering the question "Why prosper?" would be like starting an important business trip without asking where you wanted to go, why you were going, or what you wanted to experience once you got there. Prosperity, defined as an attitude, a way of being that creates a desirable world experience, requires that we know what we want and why we want it.

This is a pivotal time for women, and it is very appropriate to ask ourselves such questions as: "What do I want in life? What do I want to pursue with my time and energy that is worthwhile? What is success to me? Why do I want to prosper?"

Giving ourselves permission to prosper, to be everything that we can be, demands that we define our basic philosophy of life. When we ask "Why prosper?" we are really reflecting on the philosophical basis of our goals.

What is the bottom line for you — why do you want to prosper?

What are you trying to satisfy in your life? What motivates you to reach out and do your very best, to excel? What needs are you trying to satisfy?

We have all experienced the same existential pit of emptiness in the middle of the night that is rarely satisfied with material manifestation. Many people say that survival is the prime motivator, but do we need affluence to meet our most basic survival needs? They are easily met with a few hours of work a week. If simple survival were the goal, carrot stew is awfully cheap.

Philosopher Alan Watts claims survival is the last of our worries. He feels the existential question in life is what to do with the nine-tenths of our time that we don't need to use in working for survival.

Women are ready for something more positive than mere survival. We've had enough symbolic slaving over the hot stove and cold computer. We have no doubt about the value of our work as wife and mother — but we no longer feel limited to just this role of homemaker. We have a longing to know who we are in the bigger picture, and we have a burning in our hearts to help bring about some of the changes that are desperately needed in the world.

HAVING IT IN BALANCE

To many women, life has seemed like an either–or proposition. Either you devote your life energies to having a career and money-making activities or toward loving and serving others. We are learning that these goals are not opposites; we do not have to choose between them. The spiritual, loving path leads us through the world. Money, success, power, fame, prestige, and spirituality are all interrelated — they are our inner and outer work at one and the same time.

The human dilemma is a need to balance these two aspects of our growth — the spiritual and the pragmatic. We need to expand and reach for connection with our higher selves to feel unity and get a sense of direction. At the same time we need to "ground" our insights, and express our total selves in the day-to-day world in meaningful ways. If either dimension — the spiritual or the pragmatic — takes over, we experience crisis.

For example, the businesswoman who focuses on the "real world" of facts and figures to the exclusion of meaning and purpose in life often loses her sense of playfulness and has an inner sense of grayness, in spite of plenty of outside and financial reward.

The homemaker who overidentifies with her giving-nurturing side and devotes herself exclusively to her family is likely to sense the loss of her personal identity over time. The equilibrium is gone. She may not be aware of the inner conflict, only of being depressed and dissatisfied. She finds herself provoking arguments, being less tolerant of people and situations, and being overly critical and judgmental.

The need for balance is evident. Attaining wisdom, love, and prosperity need not be at odds — they can contribute to one another in a flow toward even greater personal growth. In other words, it is not only possible, it is also desirable, to have love, wisdom, and wealth in our lives.

But why be wealthy? Is the value of wealth only in the luxuries and leisure it affords? American essayist and poet Ralph Waldo Emerson saw prosperity in wealth and power as a natural state for human beings:

> Poverty demoralizes. . . . Men of sense esteem wealth to be the assimilation of nature to themselves. . . . Power is what they want, not candy — power to execute their design, power to give legs and feet form and actuality to their thought; which, to a clear-sighted man, appears the end for which the universe exists. . . .

SEARCH FOR WHOLENESS

Prosperity has been defined as "a state of being successful with vigorous and healthy growth." If our purpose in life is unity and harmony with all that exists, then prosperity, as an inherent element of growth, is part of our search for wholeness. To prosper is to grow, to fulfill one's destiny, to be all one can be within the context of the environment around us.

Prosperity for ourselves presupposes prosperity for all. We are all equal; there is no one among us who deserves more. The laws of prosperity are similar to the light of the sun: it shines on all alike.

How can everyone prosper? That seems to contradict everything we have ever been taught. Contrary to common belief, we do not live in a universe with limited good. Only our concepts of ourselves and of how the world is set up are limited.

If we are willing to live within the laws of the universe, the possibilities are still unlimited even in the so-called times of recession. We have only begun to tap the potential of female energy. This is our age to produce. We are part of the balance the world needs now.

Ours is not to lead or prosper by exploitation, but to balance the male's thrust in technology that has catapulted humankind to dizzying heights. As a result of the unbalanced development of this technology, for example, we have created the most fantastic destructive capabilities through nuclear weapons and guided missiles without even thinking about the total insanity of it all.

Physical force has long been extinct as a necessary survival technique, and logic alone provides a narrow view of human affairs. The intuitive, imaginative powers of the female are needed in this strife-torn world. The thinking creative male welcomes, with a sigh of relief, the new woman's willingness to share in the tremendous responsibility for creating the good life. It is for us to produce, to help create a synthesis of coexistence principles by weaving tapestries of feminine qualities of love and understanding into areas of power — government, finance, and business.

Finding our own personal and universal purpose is a life goal we must discover for ourselves before we know what part of the tapestry we can best weave. Without purpose we are lost. The joy of prosperity is only possible when we know we're on our path to self-expression.

What is it that only you can say to the world? What needs to be done that can best be done by you?

In my attempt to remind myself that there is a greater purpose to life, I keep this posted where I will see it every morning:

> Keeping in mind —
> The true nature of the universe
> The real reason for life
> The essential core of my being
> The divinity of all around me
> I rise each morning to meet the day —
> Asking to remember — all day.

PROSPERITY PROFILE NO. 2
Interview with Cheryl Wallace, a deputy public defender.

Q: How do you see yourself as a prospering woman?

A: One way in which I see myself as a prospering woman is that I've always known I can take care of myself. I've never really worried about money. Even when I was in school and I didn't have a regular job, I always had creative ways of making ends meet. There were periods of worry, but basically I have always assumed that money would be there when I needed it.

For example, I'm planning a trip to India now and the whole trip is based on faith and trust that it's going to work out. My work is to release the anxiety and focus on the trust.

Q: That's important to understand, isn't it, that we rarely see the whole trip from here to there and think it's all blossoms and honey along the way? Because that isn't the way it is. How long have you wanted to take a trip like this?

A: Since graduating from college. After finishing high school I worked as a secretary for a year, then went back to school at night. I went on to law school at night while working during the day. This process continued for two years as I studied for and passed the Bar.

In the family I grew up in, my father always assumed the money would be there, and my mother did the work to make it work. She had to put things together — make the means meet the ends. So the rules were very different with my mother carrying the financial responsibility and my father being the planner, dreamer. Now I can allow myself to take a journey like this because I learned from my dad that I can do it. Because I have no mate to handle the money issues, I've had to take on Mom's role also, and learn how to take the objective point of view of how do we do this? My personality is to hit any barrier head on. I've had to learn how to do it differently and be more flexible. I knew it was going to happen, the only question was how. I was willing to do whatever I had to do to achieve what I wanted. I was even willing to give up my place.

Q: Sometimes we have to be willing to do more than what we would like to do in order to have what we want.

A: I've learned to release myself from disappointment by letting go of my picture of what my goal — any goal — would look like in the end. By the time you get there you could say, "Oh, this is not at all how I thought it would be," and you might miss what is there.

I have no idea what to imagine about this trip. I don't believe we have the ability to know what life will be like down the road. I'm going to India to explore. It's an adventure. That's the way I want to live my life — not knowing, or thinking I need to know.

3

THE PROSPERITY PRINCIPLE —
A NEW PERSPECTIVE

"There is nothing either good or bad but thinking makes it so."
— William Shakespeare

hat if we could experience this world from a completely different perspective — a different point of view from the one most of us grew up with? What if this world is really set up for you, me, and everyone else to live happy, fulfilled lives, feeling good about ourselves, and others? That indeed would feel prosperous, wouldn't it? Yet we've all known people who have achieved prosperity in the broadest terms, whose lives seem different in that they are not struggling the way many of us are. Some of these people have discovered the *prosperity principle* — a unique attitude or point of view about life.

WHAT IS THE PROSPERITY PRINCIPLE?

The prosperity principle is a way of looking at life as if *everything happens for our benefit*. From this perspective, we learn to accept "what is" and work with it. We stop demanding that people or circumstances change in order to suit our needs and for us to be happy. We come to realize that the reason for any event in life is to learn something we need to know to take our next step in our own personal growth process.

Interpreting whatever life brings as happening for our benefit does not mean we suddenly have no problems. It also does not mean we suddenly experience no pain or anxiety in life. We do not have a choice about whether or not to have problems in life. We will always have problems. In fact, if we ever got rid of them, we would go out and get some more. Why? Because we create problems to grow by; problems are our opportunity to grow.

What does happen when we live by the prosperity principle is that we look for growth and opportunity in all experiences. Divorce, for example, may be a shattering event, but it also has the potential for positive change that possibly had been needed for a long time.

With this new perspective of looking for the lesson in "negative" events, we are able to experience emotional pain and suffering with a different attitude. We know, for instance, that emotional pain can be an alarm indicating disharmony in the mind. Pain is often triggered by fear, caused by thought. When this is happening, the pain is our signal to release fearful thought in some area of our lives.

Another outcome of living from this new perspective is learning that we cannot fail. We only choose not to go any further on a particular path. We then experience the success of choosing to let go of what is not working. From this point of view, then, our problems, barriers, and challenges are seen as opportunities to grow and we bless them accordingly.

THE SCARCITY PRINCIPLE

The scarcity principle is the opposite of the prosperity principle. To those living under scarcity, there is never enough in life: enough money, enough love, enough sex, enough power, ad infinitum. As

Auntie Mame said, "Life is a banquet, and most poor fools are starving to death!" Many people feel inadequate in themselves — incomplete — and want "something" — though they're not sure what — from others. They love in order to receive. Love becomes a barter. The only thing they have plenty of is self-doubt. To these people, success means someone else must lose, for there is only so much to go around. There are only winners and losers in their world.

Scarcity thinkers often feel that any significant movement of thought, idea, or behavior will result in a loss rather than a gain. For this reason, they rarely anticipate the future with hope. They resist change by hanging onto old ideas and behaviors, whether they bring happiness or not. After a while, getting what they truly want doesn't even enter the picture as a possibility. They rationalize by saying, "This may be bad, but at least I know what to expect." This kind of thinking keeps us in jobs, marriages, and relationships we have outgrown and yet fear letting go.

Many who are in scarcity consciousness resist change vigorously. We can't seem to get enough of what we don't really want once we think in scarcity.

One client of mine, Marie, had established a scarcity consciousness early in life, and was having difficulty giving it up when she came in to see me. Even though she was the wife of a very successful businessman, Marie was making herself miserable trying to live out her mother's image of the perfect, supportive, self-denying wife. Her frugality knew no end. She shopped the Goodwills and thrift shops for bargains on winter clothes, skimped on food, and always bought the older, bruised fruits and vegetables. As her husband's business expanded and there was plenty of money, Marie still could not spend money on herself or her family. She insisted on saving everything for a rainy day. With increasing financial prosperity, she actually became more miserable.

The rainy day had come all right — but not in the way she had anticipated. She knew how to handle poverty — but she did not know how to handle prosperity! Life was not to be enjoyed, but to be saved for.

By acknowledging her basic fears of loss that money represented to her, she was eventually able to start enjoying her money and to use it the way it was intended — as a sharing medium. As long as she focused on how little there was in life, how far it had to go around, and how difficult it was to get one's share, Marie was stuck in scarcity thinking. Even new, prosperous events are interpreted in the poverty framework when we are in scarcity consciousness.

THE NEW VIEW

How do we view life from the prosperity perspective? A prospering woman accepts the flow of life readily and adapts to unforeseen shifts. Being flexible, she is able to quickly take advantage of opportunities as life presents them. She sees change as inevitable and desirable. She is open to the endless opportunities all around her. She experiences life as living in a universe filled with abundance — and gives herself total permission to help herself to her share.

She knows that her own thoughts, attitudes, and fears limit or expand her relationship to this universal abundance. She has dreams of where she wants to go based on a realistic evaluation of herself and her environment. She has a live-and-let-live attitude toward others: cooperating, assisting when she has a choice, and deliberately choosing to focus on what is possible instead of what isn't.

Most of us slide into and out of both the consciousness of prosperity and scarcity. We are always in the process of expressing one or the other. To change scarcity thinking we need to recognize the signs of it: fear, anxiety, and worry. By releasing these emotions, we have a choice of seeing all the benefits in each situation, and gathering valuable information for the next step in our growth.

PROSPERITY PROFILE NO. 3

Interview with Dara Haskell, founder of Third Dimension Arts, Inc., a California-based company dedicated to producing and marketing Hologram wristwatches and jewelry.

Q: I know that prosperity is important to you, and you have what many might call a "prosperous life." How would you define a prosperous woman?

A: One who considers her time well spent, well remunerated. The pay could come in any form that is rewarding to the soul — whether in love, money, friendship, or other areas. One measure of rewarding work, for example, is when Monday morning is as much fun as Saturday morning — that's rewarding work.

Q: Is your work rewarding and fulfilling?

A: Definitely. I'm doing exactly what I want to do. I'm living my fantasy. I'm doing the kind of work that is well suited for me.

Nine years ago I figured out how to put holograms and watches together. Now I make hologram wristwatches and other hologram accessories. Basically I run a manufacturing process — a corporation and a factory. I'm responsible for all goods in and all goods out. Within that structure I do a lot of design work, and I do a lot of travel.

Q: And you are doing it quite successfully.

A: Yes. I'm forty-six years old and my income is over $200,000.

Q: How many people do you employ, and what is your attitude toward employees and prosperity?

A: I have between six and ten, depending on the season. These people don't quit. The last time someone quit was to retire.

I believe in paying my employees well. Once, when I had to go to an agency to get temporary secretarial help, the personnel director said my pay schedule and benefits were the best in Marin County.

I believe that if you pay people a living wage and you give them good benefits, you provide good working conditions, and you keep them happy, they have no reason to leave. Why would they want to quit? Or steal from you? I have a quarter of a million dollars worth of stock out. If my employees wanted to take it, they could. My petty cash is available too, but I've never had anything stolen.

Q: So you want prosperity not only for you, but for your employees too?

A: I want prosperity for everyone, for it makes you truly happy. I have no worries about how my financial life is going, it's not a concern for me. I know it could be. I could choose to focus on fantasies of losing my money. I don't choose to live that way.

I live a very low-stress lifestyle. I don't believe anybody should work more than forty hours a week. That's not permitted in this company. Everyone works forty hours or less; I try to work no more than thirty hours. We work very smart, and we work very hard. My secretary has worked with several other companies. She says that we put out more work in our thirty- to forty-hour week than others she has worked with put out in sixty hours.

Q: We hear so much about the effects of recession — has your business gone down?

A: The recession has hit hard in the gift and jewelry industry. Jewelry is usually one of the first to go. Our company is still doing very well. In 1992 we had a sixteen percent growth rate over 1991 and we've been able to hold our own in 1993 and 1994. One reason, I think, is that our product crosses over into many industries. Another reason the company is doing well in a recession is the way it's run, because we outperform others in our field. For one thing, we ship on time, and we ship correctly.

Q: In other words, you focus on serving.

A: Absolutely. We serve our clients. We don't focus on making money. We focus on getting the best quality product out as fast as possible. That makes us money. When you focus on making money, you have the wrong set of values.

Manufacturing is one of the most difficult businesses to be in. You not only have to make a product at a competitive price that people want to buy, which is hard enough, but you have to know your values, and keep them straight or you won't make it.

You have to be part businessperson and part psychic. You must stock the right amount at all times, and know what that amount is four to ten weeks ahead of time. You have to have enough to fill your orders, but not so much that you have it sitting around. So you have to be able to divide how much of what type of product you're going to be able to sell and to whom. In other words, your focus has to be on serving. A high percentage of manufacturing goes down from incorrect ordering.

Q: So, you acknowledge and appreciate the psychic element in business decisions.

A: I never worked in manufacturing in my life until I started this business, but somehow I was "told" and I "listened" to what needed to be done by an inner guidance.

Q: Do you accept this as normal and natural?

A: It is normal and natural for me. I run this business under the same laws that I run my spiritual life. I studied meditation for many years and learned to listen to and find the God within and above. You learn humility very quickly when you realize you're not the center of the universe. Yet, the God within gives you the inner certainty you need to run a business.

The one thing you need in business is the ability to act — act fast, act accurately. To do that you need inner strength. If you try to just come from your intellect it won't work. You must come from your intuition, which comes directly from your soul.

SUCCESSFULLY WINNING

When we experience true prosperity, we experience acceptance
by the world as worthy. This is difficult for us before
we have accepted our own worthiness.

Pesident Abe Lincoln once remarked, "People are about as happy as they decide to be." Women, too, are about as prosperous as they decide to be. Developing a life of abundance is the result of deliberate decisions. If we have traditionally blocked our prosperity consciousness with decisions which led to self-defeating attitudes about self, success, money, power, and love, then we have more work to do in the area of self-acceptance and the area of embracing life's prosperity as our deserved right.

By following the suggestions in the next four chapters, you will be able to review your belief systems and life decisions in the areas of self, success, money, power, and love, which may uncover, and so help you to change, those attitudes presently blocking your prosperity. The concept of ourselves is our first concern, for that is the basis of all other attitudes we hold.

FEMALE AND SUCCESSFUL?

The first concept to explore is whether you believe it is okay for you, as a woman, to prosper.

We have identified and celebrated masculinity with the idea of success for so long that many women have forgotten the obvious: prosperity is not gender-determined by nature. Being prosperous has nothing to do with being either female or male — it is a learned cultural role.

Once we start to challenge the limitations set by the cultural assumption that being female and successful are mutually exclusive, we are on new territory. It is no wonder, then, that one of our first concerns in becoming a prospering woman is how the men in our lives will respond to our success. We have a wide range of fears connected with this issue of invading their "domain." Some of the more effective fears we use to block our path to prosperity are such ideas as:

1. To be successful we must become masculine in attire, attitude, and behavior.
2. If we climb too high, too fast, in the business world, it will be assumed that we granted sexual favors en route.
3. As single women, our success will threaten men and we won't attract a life partner.
4. Marriage relationships will be endangered if we start to earn more money or have more prestige than our mates.

The reaction from males to our new roles is mixed. Many men totally applaud and support our more expansive roles — others don't. Because of their own fears, many men do feel threatened by the so-called new "macho woman."

It is not the attitude of men with which we need to be primarily concerned, however. Our real change in life comes from within. It is our own attitude that demands our focus. We fear the reaction of others only when we believe, at some level, that what they are saying is partially true. The key to prosperity is to change our minds — our thoughts — about ourselves and our success.

Most women do not want success to be a barrier between themselves and men. Whether it is or not will depend primarily upon our inner decisions. The challenge is to overcome our own fear of failure, fear of success, and lack of self-worth. When we feel good about our own prosperity, so will the rest of the world.

OVERCOMING FEAR OF FAILURE

When I believe my value as a human being is gauged by the results of my actions, my self-esteem is vulnerable. My fear of failing at any act is intensified.

Fear of failure is the fear of being or doing some "wrong." It presupposes there is a "right." Yet, how can we fail when there is no way of knowing, on the grand scale, the ultimate outcome of any single act we make? How many things in your life which you thought were total disasters turned out to be the best things that could possibly have happened?

Fear of failure keeps us from risking, but a willingness to risk is a measure of our prosperity consciousness. When we're blocked from this consciousness by low self-esteem, we are unwilling to try something new. Rather than be open to opportunities, we suffer from doubt and mistrust of our abilities and tie ourselves in psychological knots when faced with even the thought of stepping out, moving ahead, and taking a chance with the unknown, the unproved.

In doubt, we identify more with the possibilities of failing than of winning. We seem to be saying, "If I don't reach too high, I won't fall too far." Unconsciously, we're imagining failure far stronger than we can see, smell, or taste success.

One way out of this fear is to ask yourself, "What is the worst thing that could happen if I failed at something I really wanted? What would be the ultimate calamity?" Ask yourself if you could live with the worst possible result.

The trick is in specifying the fear. Usually the worst never happens. It rarely happens to the degree that our active imagination conjures up. By specifying the fear, however, the rational mind has something concrete to work with in helping dispel the fear. As long as the fear remains nebulous, it continues to have power over us.

Every successful person agrees that the risk is the fun of achieving. Our highs in life come not from having or surmounting any single challenge, but from the strength we experience when we find the means within us to face a challenge and overcome the barriers to resolution. Prove this to yourself by thinking back to a time in your life when you were the most elated. What challenge did you have to overcome to achieve that success? We get energy from taking a risk once we face our fear, and in spite of it. We forget that when we risk, we might lose, but we sometimes win!

Yet winning can establish a fear of its own — the fear of success can be just as paralyzing as the fear of failure.

LOOKING BENEATH THE FEAR OF SUCCESS

Have you ever felt like stopping just when things got going good? Did you feel confused about this conflict?

We all have impulses urging us to open up, move on, communicate more, give more, be more. At the same time, we can have an almost equal urge of restraint — a feeling of wanting to pull back. Why? This is often the fear of success.

Fear of success has sometimes been called the fear of the sublime — the fear of acknowledging that we really are great and wonderful beings. That idea is more than many of us can stand. Being prosperous comes too close to proving it is true.

Think how your lifestyle would change today if you truly believed that you were a great and glorious person with something valuable to contribute. How would you live? How would you act with your boss? How would you dress? What colors would you wear? What basically would be different about you? Everything we do, say, and have expresses our beliefs. An image of success could require radical change to our basic self-image that we're not ready to handle.

If success comes before the self-image is ready for it, we do whatever is necessary to put the brakes on and discredit it. When we experience true prosperity, we experience acceptance by the world as worthy. This is difficult for us before we have accepted our own worthiness.

Success also brings with it great expectations by others. It is easy to assume it is our responsibility to fulfill these expectations. Ironically this can fuel the fear of success — we may yet fail!

For example, one of my clients, Suzanne, started a wholesale catalog business and, much to her surprise, the business boomed that first year. Suzanne had never developed her sense of boundaries, and when three of her family members complained that she ought to put them on the payroll regardless of their qualifications, her joy at the business success was diminished.

There is yet another way that the fear of success is a barrier to the development of our full potential. To the degree that we fear personal success, we tend to separate ourselves from the successful. Those who dare to risk and achieve remind us painfully of what we're not doing. To avoid this pain we sometimes condemn with envy and jealousy, or we admire with awe. Both responses separate us from others.

Only when we are able to truly appreciate and enjoy the success of others are we setting up the right mental attitude to be successful ourselves. Each time we sincerely applaud others for their achievements, we can rest assured our own success is coming closer because our consciousness is on success.

Your way out of fear of success is to realize *you are in control* of your attitude. It's just as it is when you are skiing: once you know you can come to a stop, you can let go! All true success is personally defined. You decide the goal, the pace, and the parameters around which you are willing to be successful. You have only you to please in your success.

YOU ARE WORTHY

Fear of failure and success basically stems from lack of self-acceptance. Every successful woman must go through the crucial hour of facing herself squarely and declaring her own independence to herself. At that point in time, she must accept weaknesses, along with her beauty, strength, courage, and know-how. This is her moment of true liberation. It is a statement of the end of waiting in line for approval. We all know the power of self-approval. Until we reach the moment when we are able to give ourselves complete approval, however, we block our prosperity consciousness with our self-doubts and feelings of not being good enough.

Women have no edge in the market when it comes to feeling low self-esteem or feeling unworthy. It seems to come with being human. Women, however, have been considered second class for centuries, and very few of us have escaped that gnawing feeling that we'll never quite make it. This is a perfect setup for scarcity consciousness.

The prettiest are never pretty enough. Our bodies are either too big or too little in the places that count. If we don't know math, we're not smart. If we do know math, so what? It seems as though we can't win. Some of us have tried to compensate for a low self-image by being the best at everything — superwoman at home, in relationships, in school, or on the job. Too often, this only covers up those deeper feelings that somehow we have to prove ourselves to someone.

Sound familiar? It all comes from scarcity consciousness, from not feeling good enough. For whom? For ourselves, of course.

While in this state, you substitute wishing for doing. This wishing is often in the form of repetitive thoughts about ways you feel you are inadequate. How many people do you know who think that if they dwell on their faults and fears long enough:

1. This is somehow almost as good as improving?
2. Maybe some magic will happen and they will overcome their bad

habits automatically?

3. No one will criticize them because they are saying it first?
4. Someone will at least take pity on them?

What they don't realize is that by dwelling on miseries — internally and externally — they are unconsciously inviting even more negativity into their lives. The process by which this works is, paradoxically, the same process which provides the way out of low self-esteem.

Psychoanalysis focuses on the original causes of this unhealthy thinking, but if we are to get any immediate real change in behavior, we need to look beyond the root causes and focus more on how we are daily reinforcing this negative state of mind — and then concentrate our energies on the effect of finally letting go.

PROSPERITY KEY NO. 1
We reap what we sow.

Our lives manifest our dominant thoughts. Just as whatever we plant grows, that which we focus our attention on multiplies. Whatever we put into our minds comes out in our lives.

By deciding to only focus on, and move toward, what you want, you are able to raise your self-image. Each time you dwell on inadequacies, you decrease your self-assurance.

When we plant the idea in our minds that there is not enough in life, we reap scarcity. When our focus is on loss, past pain, and fear, we get more loss, pain, and suffering in return. To understand how this works, let's go a little deeper.

WE'RE ALWAYS WINNING

As author Richard Bach wrote, "Argue for your limitations, and they are yours." Some people have a life theme of believing that they can't have what they want in life — and they often don't get it. This gives the impression they are losing in life, when in fact they are winning.

This kind of winning, however, acts as a block to prosperity consciousness for it is negative winning. How does it work, and how do we remove this block? The answer is in the following key.

PROSPERITY KEY NO. 2
Proving ourselves right has its consequences.

We all have the need to be right. We want to prove that whatever we believe is in fact true. That's the nature of consciousness. If we have an unconscious low self-esteem, we will need to prove ourselves right and produce a life that supports that internal image.

It is uncanny how we mastermind a life plot that "proves" we are "no good." Depending on what the script calls for, we can: get caught, hurt ourselves, get pregnant, get fired, lose something important, overspend, get drunk, abuse those we love — whatever is appropriate to prove we're no good. When we've really proved it, we've created a win! A negative win, but a win. We showed the world we were right all along.

We select circumstances that occur in our lives by choosing how and where we focus our attention. For example, when we concentrate on reasons life doesn't work and why we can't have what we want (my husband won't like it, I don't have any money, I haven't the time, I'm too old anyway, I just can't), we remain oblivious to opportunities to change our circumstances, and so perpetuate our negative "wins" — my husband *doesn't* like it, I *don't* have any money, there *isn't* any time, and I *am* too old. In other words, our negative self-esteem and need to always be right becomes a self-fulfilling prophecy.

WINNING POSITIVELY

The law of causation is the same for both positive and negative wins. They are both produced by thought: only the emphasis is different. A positive win is created when we realize that within every problem lies a solution. It is our choice how we interpret every event. There is no one way to look at any set of circumstances.

Almost everyone has a favorite story of someone who has turned adversity into opportunity. Those who benefit from the calamities in their lives, whether it is an accident, a divorce, or a loss of some sort, are people who prefer positive wins. They create positive results from even the negative circumstances of life by choosing to focus on what they *want* and on what they *can* do.

As long as we are content to substitute negative wins (proving that we can't) for positive wins (proving that we can) we effectively block our prosperity consciousness. Before we are able to move out of low self-esteem and give up negative wins, however, we must recognize the "payoffs," or benefits we receive in them. The single biggest payoff for negative wins is getting to play the "martyr," and we will go to great lengths to play that game. For example, when we stay with an alcoholic mate who has no intention of changing, we may be expressing a need to be put down, a need to feel like the "healthy one" in a relationship, or a need to perform the miracle of changing another person. We may have an ax to grind, such as choosing men who reject us, and thus prove that all men are brutes, or we need to prove that we're unlovable.

If we assume that all life is growth-oriented, we would have to agree that we are always moving toward the expansive, the positive. We choose whatever we think is best every moment, according to our state of conscious awareness. The basic underlying reason for every act then is good — only the means create the negative results. The more conscious we become about who we are in relation to all life, the more directly we can get what we want in a positive manner.

If we are all moving toward the positive, then why don't we believe what our own eyes and ears tell us about the negative situations we're in? Because, unconsciously, until we get the "message" in the negative situation, we will do whatever is necessary to remain in the learning situation!

We repeat our negative wins until we're clear about what we want, or at least don't want. Then we are ready — with energy built from the experience — to go on to our next step. We change internally so we can tolerate a different life externally.

The sooner you can find your payoff in any negative situation, the sooner you can speed up this learning process. Once you become aware of the name of the game you're playing, the easier it is to let it go. This frees you to get on with positive wins.

Use this prosperity key of always proving yourself right to identify any negative self-image you may be "proving." Look at every negative situation as if you were winning — *somehow* — even if it is difficult to see how this could be. *Do not blame yourself.* Ask yourself, "How is this a win for me? What am I getting out of this that I couldn't get faster any other way?"

As soon as you give yourself permission to prosper, step through your fears of failure and success, see that you deserve all that you desire, and move toward what you want, rather than toward what you don't want, you are deciding to win successfully!

PROSPERITY PROFILE NO. 4
Interview with Vera Topinka, a Mill Valley photographer
who specializes in portraits and business profiles.

Q: Vera, I see you living a prosperous life. Would you describe yourself as a prospering woman?

A: The thing that comes up for me is that I feel prosperous according to the amount of joy and aliveness that I feel in my life on a daily basis. That became really clear to me recently when I was able to have an incredible experience. Every moment of one full day and night I was in a total sense of aliveness and joy.

Q: Could you define what you were doing that allowed you to be in that state of grace?

A: I really wasn't doing anything different. I was just naturally doing things I ordinarily do, but in an altered state. I felt incredible aliveness coursing through my body — that state that makes you smile and laugh without any reason — a sense of being present every moment. I felt both engaged and an observer at the same time.

Q: It sounds like the kind of state some people try to get from taking drugs, yet I'm assuming this experience occurred without drugs.

A: Yes, totally — absolutely naturally. It showed me that whatever I'm doing, I'm on the right path. This is my goal — my vision statement — and I experienced the possibilities of how I want to live my life every day.

Q: What are some of the pieces of learning that helped you get on this path?

A: I've learned to train my mind. It is when my mind is being negative that I'm miserable. When I'm uplifted and looking for the highest thought, then I'm okay. I have been practicing that with friends for a whole year. I have been meeting with them for two hours once a week. We focus on spirit, goals, changes we go through, realizations we have. This has been so important in the changes I have been able to make.

Also, I have always been pretty athletic — I'm outdoors a lot. This is an important part of who I am. Nature is responsible for my being able to appreciate everything. In nature, there is a system of orderliness, a system of incredible beauty that seems to just nurture your soul. And being out in it often seems to have an accumulative effect.

Q: What role does money play in your life of joy?

A: I've made some wonderful changes regarding money. I've learned to turn it over to my spirit. On my vision chart I've put myself in a state of joy in the middle of this dollar bill. That's how I want to live my life — that's my goal. Educating myself about money is something I will continue to do the rest of my life. It was a major lack in my education.

Q: I do know that the way you've chosen to spend your money is unique in that you see prosperity as being free.

A: Prosperity doesn't mean anything to me if I don't get to play a lot. If I don't have a lot of time off then, in my eyes, I'm not successful. This is not to say I don't like my work. I love my work. There is way more to life than the work I do. As a photographer, I love the interaction with people. I feel so lucky to have found what for me is right livelihood. However, there are mountains to climb and rivers to run, bikes to ride, love to make, and friends to hang out with. I'm not going to wait until I've retired to do this; I want to live my life this way now. And for me it's about trusting there will be enough money whether or not I take my one week off a month to do other things, which is what I do now.

Q: What do you do during your time off?

A: It's just remarkable what happens when you don't schedule work for a whole week! So many wonderful opportunities come up — I can go to a lake by myself or to Wilbur Hot Springs to soak up solitude for four days, just be with the spirit and envision my life. I often spend days not talking to anyone. I just love it. The more quiet I get, the more in touch with intuition I am, and the more I know how to design my life. Almost all my good ideas come from that kind of introspection. If I don't get away to places that are not distracting, then I begin to think I have to live my life the way everybody says I have to live it — which is not for me. The more I listen to the quiet, the more I listen to what really is for me.

I'm not rich. I don't own my own house yet. I don't have a lot of trappings that people feel mean wealth. I do feel lucky. I have a house to live in that I really love. I have work that is wonderful, friends with whom I can be intimate. I do enjoy driving around in my car with the top down, so I have a few toys. There are other toys I want, like a boat so I can go out on the bay. Essentially though, I am learning to live more simply because what I'm after is deep fulfillment in my life. My questions to myself are "How do I need to live my life in order to feel deeply fulfilled every minute of my life? What do I need to be in touch with to do that?" To some degree, it has to do with money. I just trust that the money will be there, and so far it has been.

More importantly, I am starting to become aware of which activities deeply satisfy me and which don't. For example, going out for an expensive meal doesn't do it for me. I'd rather meet in my friend's home and make dinner together, or pack up a lunch and go for a hike up the mountain. That's where the intimate conversations that I really enjoy can take place. Society is always telling us what will make us happiest — I just want to figure it out for myself.

Q: It doesn't sound like you are avoiding negative feelings.

A: No. I have a lot of empathy and I feel great sadness when things happen in life. In the past, I think I used to avoid the hurting feelings. But, when you learn to feel that inner joy, you have all the other feelings available too. My childhood wasn't perfect, but I knew joy. I've always known that my true nature is joy. I was born with it. That's how I know now if I'm on my path or not. When I'm not feeling joyous for days in a row, I've lost it, and I have to take a look and see where I went off the path and correct my course.

5

MONEY IS THE MEANS

Everything reflects our consciousness, and there is
little value in staying in the consciousness of poverty.

Prosperity has had only one connotation for too long — money. In previous chapters we have redefined prosperity in more holistic terms; now let's take a new look at what money is.

The subject of money has a powerful emotional charge, equivalent to the subject of sex. Yet, we will usually talk about it only like the weather — in general economic terms. In this age of open discussion on homosexuality, menstruation, and incest, it is interesting that we are still very closed in what we reveal about our money. The subject of our inner feelings concerning money is one of the last things to come out of the closet. Why?

When we think of having money, we think of opportunities for independence, leisure, privacy, time to do and act as we wish. Unfortunately, a lack of money translates into yet another reason to put ourselves down.

We have built a complex of myths and voodoo around the idea of money as an entity — an end in itself. We have personified it, and attributed characteristics to it as if it were a savior. How many times have we said, "If only I had enough money!" At the same time, we have created a concept of money as an active, negative agent. We have done this through our conscious and unconscious myths which support a negative morality system about what money does to people. We end up both desiring and fearing money.

I can remember a time when I didn't want to talk about money, or even think about it. I felt squeamish asking for money due to me. And in establishing a price for anything, I always hoped that somehow the other person just "knew" how much was fair so we would not have to discuss it. I even fancied what it would be like to live in a community of total barter so no money would have to be exchanged.

It wasn't until later that I found out I wasn't alone — many people are uneasy when they must receive, ask for, and speak of money. Fortunately, there are different ways of looking at money: what it is and isn't, what it can and can't do. Examining our concepts of money can open up issues concerning giving and taking that are important in all aspects of our lives.

The basis for understanding and being comfortable with money is just one more aspect of our self-awareness. For example, from repeated studies in human behavior, we know that one of the factors by which we judge ourselves and others is money — how much we make, how we make it, and how we spend it. This constitutes part of our market value. To many of us, then, speaking of income is really speaking of our value in society.

When we have a low self-image, we sometimes try to compensate for these feelings both by trying to increase our value and by trying to keep this value hidden. We want to avoid facing a low opinion from others if our value figure is not as high as we think it should be.

An example of wanting to hide our value is deciding not to invite people to dinner because we have only mismatched glasses and china. When we are devaluing ourselves because of a lack of money, we may feel ashamed at gatherings of friends of family who talk about travel, shopping, or prestigious colleges for the kids. We may put our-selves down because we don't have the money to shop or travel, or because our kids are only going to work, instead of college.

THE MORALITY OF MONEY

The self-esteem and money issue is further confused by the rather shaky image of what having that green stuff means. Although every-one wants more money, the idea of having wealth is tainted. On one side of the coin, money is thought to be highly desirable; on the other side, it is considered bad and almost dirty.

Most of the cultural arguments that make prosperity a moral issue are never made out loud. The ideas that we can't or shouldn't be financially prosperous are projected subliminally in the form of myths or beliefs. Whether we live it or not, one of our strong beliefs is that hard work and toil are rewards in and of themselves. It is also part of our tradition that poverty is a virtue. Certain religious teachings from the Bible have even been interpreted as confirming that poverty is somehow holy.

For example, the biblical passage, "Blessed are the poor in spirit, for theirs is the kingdom of heaven," has been frequently quoted to condemn wealth and praise poverty. With better understanding of the old Arabic translations, however, new interpretation among biblical scholars shows that the original intention of this and other passages was positive. With new research, we now know the word poor origi-nally meant humble and receptive, not poverty-stricken. To receive is to open oneself to one's vulnerability — to let go of control. The mes-sage seems to have been that the world is full of givers; what we need to learn is to receive — to open ourselves to our vulnerability.

Other biblical passages, such as, "It is easier for a camel to go through the eye of a needle than for a rich man to enter the kingdom of heaven," have been used to prove that being wealthy is morally wrong. According to modern-day scholars, this passage originally referred not to having money itself but rather to the difficulties inherent when we are controlled by our possessions rather than being in control of them.

Everything reflects our consciousness, and there is little value in staying in the consciousness of poverty. Someone has remarked that the best thing we can do for the poor is not to be one of them. This is not being unloving. It is a statement of not accepting poverty as inevitable. Poverty helps no one.

Other biblical passages point out another, more prosperous attitude toward life:

> Ask and it shall be given you;
> Seek and ye shall find;
> Knock, and the door shall be opened unto you.

Environmental support for the negative attitudes we hold about wealth is found in clichés we often hear repeated:

> Money is the root of all evil.
> Money won't buy you happiness.
> Easy come, easy go.
> I may be poor, but I'm happy.

I'm sure you can recite many more. They imply that not only is there something wrong with money, but, by implication, there may be a lot more wrong with *you* if you have it!

WHAT IS MONEY REALLY?

Money is commonly defined as a medium of exchange. What we are exchanging is *energy*. Money is a concept symbolizing the exchange of potential energy. It is stored energy made visible.

It is obvious that, like everything else, money is in itself neither good nor bad. It is neither moral nor immoral. To look at money as a moral issue is as absurd as it is to decide that airplanes are good or bad. We feel differently about airplanes when they are used to drop napalm bombs than when they are used to drop food supplies for starving people. Yet they are the same planes. The moral issue is in the intention of the user — not in the plane itself. Money can be used to promote life and love, and can be a blessing for many, or it can be used to destroy the life force in a million different ways.

LOVING MONEY

Accumulation of wealth has long meant having more than one's share, and gaining at the expense of others. We are reminded of the Robber Barons of all ages — companies and individuals whose assets are the result of exploitation. The get-rich-quick'ers with a "to hell with the means" attitude have poisoned our minds about money with the beliefs that (1) what one has to do to gain wealth is to steal, and (2) wealth (i.e., greed) ruins the human soul. When we point to those who misuse money selfishly as proof that money is bad, we are confusing the pirate with his ship.

A ship is indifferent as to who is at its wheel. It responds just as swiftly to a scoundrel as to a saint if both are equally skilled in the laws of sailing. Carefully loaded, its hull will carry contraband arms to thieves just as safely as it would emergency medical supplies to a disaster area. Ships, like money, are just there to be used as resources. How some people in the past have used them does not change their value.

When we are prospering naturally, we are using a holistic approach to achievement within a "win-win" position. We do not need to rely on taking from or exploiting others. With this kind of prosperity, loving money is loving the good it can do for us, and for everyone else. Prosperity in this sense is appreciating money as a means for exchanging good for all.

MONEY AS POWER

Money brings power. Money has no power in itself, but having control over how it will be spent gives us power. The more money we have, the more potential power we have.

The eighteenth-century German poet Goethe said, "Nobody should be rich but those who understand it." His point is that many can become prosperous quickly, but not always develop awareness, scruples, or concern for others. They can lose their money just as quickly, or in some way pay dearly for it, if they do not develop their prosperity consciousness.

If we are going to ask for power in great amounts, we had better be prepared to handle it. An example of what happens when we are unprepared for the power of money emerged during a recent follow-up study of the million-dollar lottery sweepstakes winners in Canada. The vast majority of them were broke within five years. Their prosperity consciousness was not developed to the point where they could benefit from the money for very long. You will either control or be controlled by money. Awareness of the power of money and of how to handle it makes the difference. It is the conscious choice to use money benevolently that puts you in control.

MONEY AS RESPONSIBILITY

The stored energy that money symbolizes is there to help us grow. This energy must keep moving. Effectively directing this movement of energy requires an understanding of how the laws of prosperity operate in giving, receiving, spending, and saving. Responsibility of money is knowing where we want to go with this energy.

PROSPERITY KEY NO. 3
To receive more, we must be willing to give more.

Money doesn't grow by being hoarded. Hoarding is for beggars. It doesn't benefit anyone to grab as much as possible and keep it stashed away in vaults or coffee cans. Trying to prosper by bottling up money through accumulation will result in the opposite negative effect. We hear tragic stories of those individuals who die each year in poverty with their "wealth" stuffed in their mattresses. It served no one, least of all them.

In all of life, receiving depends upon giving. There are no separate rules for money. All spending is part of the circulating flow of giving — when done in the right spirit. Try it out. Next time you spend, see yourself as giving to benefit others as well as yourself. Spending with love can be a new experience. Just as work can be love in action so, too, money can be love expressed. When we give in this spirit, our return is multiplied many times.

Spending is no problem for some people. It can be too easy, in fact. After a few experiences of succumbing to the temptation of unlimited credit, leading eventually to unlimited debt, they quickly discover the pain of overspending, of being out of balance at the other end of the spectrum.

Part of the responsibility that goes along with the power of money is knowing how to save and invest for a purpose. Poet Ralph Waldo Emerson, for example, saw money as a "stewardship," or challenge. To him, each person with money has a mandate to use that money to "carve out" work for others.

How do you use money? What plans or direction do you see for your money? What seeds are being planted with your money?

If the farmer has no plan, and throws her seeds hither and yon, she not only wastes her resources, she has only a small crop in return. And she cannot tend her crop if it is scattered. Start planning for your future now by investing in yourself. Spend some time today thinking about how you feel about money. Ask yourself:

Are you willing to create the money your life dream would cost?
What does "being poor" mean to you? How does that feel?
How do you feel about wealthy people?
How do you feel about earning "a lot" of money?
How do you want to receive your money?

How do you want to help others with your money?

How are you uncomfortable around money?

What do you want to have achieved with your money when you die?

Far too many people never sit down and think concretely about these kinds of questions; yet, for prosperity, it is vital to know your feelings about money. How do you feel when you spend money? Pay attention the next time when you pull out your wallet or checkbook — are you spending from a sense of loss or giving? Listen to what you are saying to yourself as you hand out money.

What is your attitude about giving? When is it easiest to give? When is it hardest to give? Listen to the clichés ringing in your ears during your transactions with money. Our attitudes toward money are often indicative of our attitudes toward life itself. Do you give freely of yourself? Is it hard for you to receive?

In order to achieve prosperity on a continuous basis, we must develop *balance*. Momentary desires will have to be balanced with long-term goals; savings, spending, and investing plans will have to be devised. Prosperity requires planning, clear intent, and commitment. Becoming friends with money and recognizing what it can and cannot do for us is an important preliminary step.

Money in itself cannot make us happy, but with intention it can provide the means of unlimited good for ourselves and others.

PROSPERITY PROFILE NO. 5

*Interview with Jana Janus, a graphic artist and entrepreneur
who moved to communist Russia to establish Alpha Graphics,
a quick-print shop in Moscow that provides people
with fax, photocopying, and printing services.*

Q: You've traveled extensively since I last talked to you, and you're living in Russia now. Tell me what your definition of a prospering woman is now.

A: In l987 I had a nice little business and real abundance was starting to show up in my life, but I had this big question: Does my philosophy only work here where everything is affluent and easy, or could it actually travel? That was a burning question — was it real — would it transfer? When I decided to move to Russia it was still a communist Russia, more commonly referred to now as the former Soviet Union.

Q: Define your philosophy.

A: First of all, it's my whole way of thinking. I learned long ago that my thoughts create my reality. Not in a cut-and-dried way. I don't sit and think I'll create a million dollars — it doesn't work like that. It's a system of thought much like a mandala. There are many parts to it; it's a center focal point and off that point are a lot of different things — that's a pulsation of my life — that's what my thinking is about. Even as I focus in on something there are a lot of parts to it. There is always a lot more than just one little thing going on.

Q: For example, prosperity is not just about money?

A: Absolutely — that's part of it. It's such a system, a mandala, that you cannot remove any one part of it. It's all things together. That's been a very deep discovery for me. There is more vitality in each thing in life.

The main point is managing thought — that's the bottom line in life. Our thoughts, left to run on their regular tracks, do all kinds of things. For example, if someone looks at you in what you consider a strange way, you begin your interpretation. I have really worked at letting go of interpretation. It's freedom! I don't worry about what you're thinking. You'll tell me, or I will ask you. If I have a concern, I will ask you, "Ruth, is there something bothering you?" And you will tell me, and I will take you at your word. It's enough for me. It never used to be enough.

Q: You stopped trying to psych out the other person, or expect the other to know what you are thinking.

A: Yes. I've learned to tell you what is on my mind. Many years ago, I wrote a story about a garden. This garden had weeds, and oh, there was such a flurry about how to get rid of those weeds. That was 1968. I'm a flower gardener. I acknowledge a weed when I see it, but I don't give it attention, I don't water it; I pull it out and lay it aside. I am not willing to think on, and put my precious thought on it. Thought is so powerful. It's it! Most people are weed gardeners. And yet they worry all the time because their garden is full of weeds.

I say, "Don't water the weeds. Acknowledge that they are there. You want a flower in your garden? You see one nice flower — you have one good thought — maybe about something nice someone did — water that thought." Why make minimal the positive things? I don't feel like I am like a Pollyanna — I am a realist.

Q: This difference between this approach and just positive thinking is that you recognize the weeds and you pull them up, you do something — you're action-oriented.

A: Total action. Thought management has been the critical thing for me. It's at the base of all my success. You can't imagine the negativity I encountered in communist Russia. The country was a nation of victims — and with good reason they believe that! It's not that they don't have good reason, but you can't go anywhere being a victim.

My question was, "Can I affect a reality in such a place?" It's one thing to sit here in the United States thinking about creating success and peace of mind — but do these ideas transfer? Will they work elsewhere?

Q: What happened?

A: Well, what do you know — it's worldwide — this stuff works. I needed to know that — to see these thoughts work in business. For example, take my participation in the beginning of the first quick-print shop in Moscow, Alpha Graphics, print shop of the future — that's the motto. To be able to open the door to the people to have access to fax machines, photocopiers, printing presses — it was a thrill to see Russian businesses getting business cards. They loved it. This was a Soviet-Canadian joint venture with an American franchise opened in hard currency.

We opened an exact replica of their stores around the world, in Tucson, New York, anywhere, and we opened it right there on Gorky Street — paint, carpet, everything. People were astounded.

But the Russian people could not use the service because it was based on hard currency. So it was an example of apartheid, but I came from a different point of view. All the equipment was bought with hard currency. The ruble had an artificial value. Russians would stare. It was like having a party in someone's house and the family was not entitled to come. It's a strange feeling.

I was able to train an apprentice. The woman left after two years and started her own business — which is a natural progression in the U.S. I'm very proud of Julia and take pride in her contribution — and look forward to seeing how far she'll take it.

Q: Who did you service?

A: We serviced embassies. Before we opened, all the joint venture businesses from the Western world could not find the kind of service they needed. I had to constantly be on guard because negative thinking was prevalent in the former Soviet Union. And I see why. I can't begin to describe the conditions under which the people have to live.

I helped to bring personal growth seminars to Russia and tried to enroll people by telling them they have choice, but taking personal

responsibility for one's happiness was almost beyond their compre-
hension. Choice was a very big issue. They had no experience of personal power, and all the systems supported that view. Self-esteem was
under the floorboards. Victims were everywhere.

Many people who took the seminars ended up quitting their jobs.
Most of the employment was under the old system. Very few people
were employed doing anything they enjoyed doing. After the training
they began to think in terms of choosing what they really wanted to
do. This was a country that penalized people for changing jobs. In
communist Russia you had an employment book, like a passport —
that official. When you worked for an organization you deposited
your book there and, if they took a dislike to you, they could put bad
marks in your book that would stick to you the rest of your life. So
people were never willing to make any waves because of the heavy
penalties, and those black marks never erased. Also, if you changed
employment, it was very bad, and very difficult to find work.

Q: A way of controlling.

A: Total control. People were very intimidated. They would live their
whole lives in the most boring jobs because of the fear of the black
mark that would stay with them.

Now they are changing — that's not the system anymore. There's
no going back. It would be like stuffing the baby back in the womb
— the baby's in the world. The gates have opened.

When I first went to communist Russia I had an image that all
these big apartment houses were like nests with all these baby birds
expecting Mother Russia to feed them, while they sat there helpless.
They all need to be kicked out of the nest. Some will fly and some
won't, but they can't live their whole lives in a nest, and that was what
was happening there. They had had all their decisions taken away.

Q: They had been taught not to fly away?

A: Yes. God forbid. They were given examples of dead birds all over the floor. After all, Stalin did kill 40 million people — that's a good example of a powerful image of why you should not distinguish yourself and why you should keep your mouth shut.

There are a lot of Westerners in Russia now, and the Western consciousness in helping to bring change. A Westerner is very noticeably different. For example, with me, it's not a question of, "Can I do it?" If I want to do it, I do it! I don't have a lot of limitations on me. When I was asked if I could raise $100,000 to begin a newspaper — gulp, then I had to say, "I think I can do it." I knew I could put energy into that, and focus, and I knew I could get damn close to the goal. I am extremely "California" in that way. I found a lot of support in California for that kind of thinking.

That's what I bring with me to this new country. I have a driver — a woman driver who is also my housekeeper. I don't tolerate her saying, "Oh, I don't think I can; it is so difficult." I press into her a concept of what she can and can't do. I tell her, "I can. Is something different about you?" She no longer gives me excuses. I only ask her to do what needs to be done — not jump off the roof. Here's a good example: I live in a Russian building; I'm the only foreigner in the building. Each section has an entrance — all pretty grimy — it looks like you're going into the projects — graffiti and filth everywhere. The fluorescent light tube went out in the foyer. It is pitch black in there, with no windows to bring in light. I said, "Irena, you must find who is in charge and get that light changed." She said, "Oh no, those are hard lights to find." I said, "Irena, it's a fluorescent light. There are millions of fluorescent lights here. They exist." She said, "Oh, I don't think . . ." I said, "You go to whoever is in charge and you tell him that whatever it takes we want that light operating." They will never make demands like that; they will accept everything. They don't like to make a commotion. This is called a commotion — this is very assertive.

So, Irena went to the man and returned saying, "Oh no, they don't have any light." I said, "There are lights. I know there are lights.

You tell him I will pay for this light — wherever this light is, I will pay for it." She went back — two days later we had light.

Q: Did you have to pay for it?

A: No, they just knew that this was not going to slide with me. I just kept at it each day — I said, "This is dangerous, it is pitch dark, there could be anybody lurking in there. This is not acceptable." I refused to accept it — that was the key. I would have figured out how to get a light bulb, even if I had to go to a State organization and offer them money to take a tube out of one of their own lights. It wasn't a question of sitting around. I was going to have light in that hallway. That was a given.

Q: That's empowerment at work, is it not?

A: This woman is wonderful. She used to be so scared of making a mistake. She has gained enormous courage.

POWER, RESPONSIBILITY, AND PROSPERITY

"Whatever you can do, or dream you can, begin it.
Boldness has genius, power, and magic in it."

— Goethe

Prospering women are powerful women; they have made friends with their personal power. They did not become strong; they acknowledged the strength they already had.

Personal power is not aggressive, muscular, manipulative, or authoritative power, but an inner power that comes from knowing we have all the resources we need to handle whatever comes our way in life. When we have personal power we shift from the pseudo-strength of appearing strong to the real strength of feeling strong. An example of this for me is being confronted with criticism from powerful men I admire, and being able to remain objective. It is a personal victory every time I do not cringe in self-blame, or feel the need to lash back at "unjust" criticism in a defensive manner. When I'm coming from a sense of my own personal power, I can listen, be open to the truth that is coming through, and release the rest.

With this inner strength to face our challenges, life is accepted on its own terms. With personal power we engage in the dance without having to be the choreographer. Coming from strength, whatever happens is okay because we're okay.

Women have always had the potential for all the personal power they needed. They have always been strong; they had to be. By withstanding the centuries of being told they were the weaker, ineffectual, dependent, nonassertive half of the human population, they proved their strength. Even in the face of these charges, women have always known, deep down, they were capable, strong, smart, assertive, rational, and decisive.

The only change in the power of women is that now we are beginning to acknowledge this strength and take it, en masse, into a world where male mindsets and philosophies still prevail. We are making that leap from experiencing "inner strength" to accepting responsibility for our lives.

With that leap in consciousness we are rejecting the "trickle-down" economic theory we all grew up with. Under that theory many women believed that men had power by nature and that women would benefit most by pleasing the men in their lives. In this way, a woman was encouraged to seek power through osmosis — to be content with the power achieved through association with a strong male.

One reason this theory has lasted so long is that women focused on the benefits and ignored the consequences. It felt good to think there was someone wiser and stronger who could always answer the questions and take away the pain.

Obviously, there are several major flaws in this co-dependent system. For one thing, we hand out fistfuls of energy to anyone we allow to have control over us. Psychologist John Enright uses an analogy of the trained falcon to illustrate living under the illusion of powerlessness when operating from dependency. The falcon, after making a strike, always returns its prey to the master and then gratefully accepts its small strip of flesh from the kill as reward. Dependency has been trained into the bird until freedom is forgotten, and the source of food is associated only with the master. When we become dependent, we forget that we are our own source.

We also give away power to those we feel are superior to us. The world as we see it is only a reflection of who we are. In order to see admirable characteristics in others, we must already have them in ourselves. We are potentially all that we admire; there is no need for females or males to deny personal power and separate themselves as superior or inferior beings.

The second major flaw in the trickle-down, power-through-association theory of female-male relationships is that women lose their decision-making power when they deny responsibility for themselves, for the two go hand in hand.

In this period of transition when women and men are finding new paths together, many women want the freedom to make decisions and still be protected and provided for. The answer seems to lie in women releasing fear of personal power within themselves.

PERSONAL POWER — HOW TO GET IT

Prosperity means experiencing more choice in life. But choice only has meaning when we have the power to handle the consequences of our choices. Handling consequences demands that we have a sense of personal power. How do we invert our personal power? By having integrity, intention, and by taking responsibility.

(1) Personal power is dependent upon having a strong sense of integrity.

The root meaning of integrity is to act as one. When we act from integrity, our desires and actions are aligned. The power that comes from acting with integrity can be likened to the power of a group pulling a rope in one direction, versus split action by the same group pulling in different directions. We have much more "pull" when the desires of our body, mind, and feelings are integrated.

Personal power comes from within and depends upon you

approving of you. Your approval comes from your sense of integrity —
a total honesty within yourself. It means being who you are without
pretense — acting on what you truly feel. When you live with integrity, your actions, words, and intentions are congruent with your values.
You believe what you are saying and doing. Lack of integrity creates a
sieve out of your pot of personal power.

(2) *Being honest about intentions with yourself and others is a basic
ingredient of personal power.*

Keeping agreements is an example of being honest with oneself.
For instance, there is always a good "excuse" for being late to work or
to an appointment. Even when the other person accepts your excuse,
however, you feel an internal "scrunch." You know the truth that you
could have made it had your intention been clear. If the appointment
had been the last possible time to receive a free $10,000 bonus, you
would have made it on time! Pay attention to how you feel the next
time you give an excuse. No matter how good you are at acting justi-
fied, you devalue yourself inside when you don't keep your word,
and your sense of integrity drops. Our energy contracts rather than
expands when our integrity drops, so less integrity means less power.

Personal power is increased by becoming clearer in our intentions. As we get hungry for more power, we quickly learn the importance of saying yes only to those agreements we intend to keep. This
plugs some of the holes of that sieve fast.

(3) *Taking responsibility is a third way to increase personal power.*

If we live as though the world is against us, we don't experience
much power. If we want increased power, we must assume responsibility for what we do, and don't do, in every situation.

Being able to take responsibility has long been considered a male
attribute — and one that often seemed more a burden than a blessing.

Many women now recognize the hidden "goody" behind taking responsibility is that you have more power as the decision maker. The interrelation of power, responsibility, and prosperity can simply be stated as "the buck stops here!" This next prosperity key tells us how to embrace our personal responsibility.

PROSPERITY KEY NO. 4
Our Personal Power Formula is:
$$E = MC^2$$
(Energy comes from seeing my contribution in every situation.)

When I take *responsibility* for the circumstances of my life, I am acknowledging that I created those circumstances. The more responsibility I accept for the consequences of my actions, the more power I am assuming. I did it, so if I don't like the results, I can redo it. The more power I accept over all circumstances of my life — as consequences of my actions — the more prosperous situations I can *choose* to create.

Responsibility is a position — an attitude toward events. You either take responsibility, or you feel victimized by the world. Your choice of whether to play the victim or to take responsibility, that is, acknowledge your contribution or part in any given situation, will determine whose power grows — yours or someone else's. If you take the position of victim, you lose power. If you choose responsibility, you have power then to do something about what's happening — to choose your next step. For example, if you take responsibility for your husband's leaving you (when you didn't want him to), you are psychologically free to look at the ways you helped set up the relationship so he would want to leave. You then learn quickly what you don't want to do next time, and you benefit from the experience.

THE SELF-DEFEATING NATURE OF BLAME

In the past we have blocked our prosperity consciousness by rejecting responsibility because we confused it with blame. When we're stuck in "victim consciousness" we often refuse to assume responsibility because we think, "If I'm responsible, then I am to blame" or, conversely, "If I take responsibility, then the other person gets off scot-free."

Blame has no place in prosperity thinking. Blame is only a judgment superimposed on the event. We blame when we're angry at ourselves for feeling stuck. Blame leads only to further blame. Look at areas in your life where you may still be holding anger and blame. You will need to decide if you are willing to let go of these negative feelings for your own benefit.

For example, parents have always been the recipients of our blame. Few of us want to acknowledge we had much to do with our own upbringing. The myth we try to perpetuate is that our parents are the reasons why we aren't the sweetest, nicest, most generous, lovable creatures imaginable. If our parents had only been halfway what we "needed" them to be, we would probably have been president by now — or at least not nearly as neurotic. We often feel ruined for life by what our parents did or did not do in raising us.

As long as we sing this old, sad song — true or untrue — we are cutting ourselves off today from our power far more effectively than Mom or Dad could have ever done.

It is time to get on with life, and the way to do it is to assume responsibility.

Without blaming yourself or your parents, you gain in power every time you can identify the choices you made in attitude and behavior and the benefits you received from your formative life.

One way out of this negative, blaming cycle is to pretend, just pretend, you chose your parents. If this crazy idea were true, what benefits would you have received from your choice? What lessons did you learn fast? In what way are you a better person from having learned these lessons? This is the type of responsible thinking that allows you to release a negative, blaming attitude.

We have the choice of experiencing the temporary power that comes with acting from anger and blame, or we can recognize the pain of a particular situation, look at what we did to help create the situation, and put our energy instead into positive planning for moving toward what we want now.

As we begin to take responsibility for ourselves, to follow the $E=MC^2$ key, we are more open to signs and signals from our environment giving us better directions. Our senses are activated as we open up to our intuition. With more complete information and increased personal power we automatically make better decisions. Because of this, we are now ready to start creating a world that fits us better.

PROSPERITY PROFILE NO. 6
Interview with a medical doctor who wishes to remain anonymous.

Q: The sexual and mental abuse many women have experienced as children is finally being brought out of the closet, and the devastating effects can no longer be denied. I know that you've not only faced that abuse but you've done something about it. You have learned to prosper by taking responsibility in this area of your life, as well as in other areas. What does taking responsibility mean to you — especially around the abuse you suffered as a child?

A: Elisabeth Kübler-Ross reminded us in listing the five stages of grieving — denial, anger, bargaining, depression, acceptance — that denial is the first stage. Denial gives us time to be able to handle what the awareness is going to bring. Some of us women in our thirties and forties are having the childhood memories of sexual abuse that we have denied until now because we simply couldn't handle the memories. Along with the memories come the locked emotions that naturally come up. I'm sure that's how it was with me.

What I initially did was say, "Oh well, my parents had a rough life," and sort of went right directly to "It's okay." I didn't acknowledge anger, so I didn't have it available for my life. I needed to retrace my steps and allow myself to acknowledge the truth that I was angry at how I was treated.

When I read that people who were abused as children had an increased predisposition of perpetuating the cycle, I was frightened. I'm sure that knowledge affected my decision about having children because I didn't want to do that. I was worried that it was programmed into me and I would unconsciously carry it out.

As my first act of taking responsibility, I entered my own therapy of doing inner child work. I found out that, in fact, I was carrying out the program — on myself. My inner parent was abusing my inner child through the critical way I had developed of speaking to myself. I saw what a harsh environment I was living under — and how I was not leaving much room for play and spontaneity. I found that I had no permission to feel all my feelings — that negative feelings were not allowed.

I learned to grieve the childhood I didn't have. It wasn't all good or bad — we're always on a continuum of functionality — but I found my child very sad. When I first did visualization of my inner child she wouldn't even look at me. She was very closed, stiff. With time, love, and patience I've been able to contact that part of me and stop the self-abuse I had learned.

Part of taking responsibility involved becoming more self-aware. I used to constantly think, "Why did you do that? Something must be wrong with you!"

Q: Assuming something was wrong with you.

A: Right. Blaming myself. I was always looking for the right answer, thinking then I would be okay. I learned first to take responsibility for grieving the child within me that had taken on all this blame.

Then I had the realization that some of the inner problems I was facing came from learned patterns. They didn't start and end with me. They were multigenerational — they weren't just from my family of origin; they probably applied to my grandparents' generation, as well as their parents'. I realized that to break this cycle takes a great amount of energy — it would be a real endeavor, a challenge of the first magnitude. I knew also that if my patterns were learned, they could be unlearned. I could learn how to live my life a different way.

One of the major issues for me was boundaries and limits — appropriate limit setting. With the history I had of physical, emotional, and sexual abuse, I didn't know how to say no. I'm still working on that; I think it's a lifelong journey.

Q: But you find yourself getting better at it?

A: Definitely. I'm not numb anymore, so my pain can be my compass now. Before, my emotions were not available to me — I didn't know when someone was invading my boundaries and that it wasn't okay with me. So getting in touch with anger has been very helpful as a signal for more appropriate responses.

I feel it's equally important to not get stuck in anger — to be able to move through it. I'm not certain how that happens. There seems to be a certain amount of charge that needs to be released. Once I was willing to acknowledge it, and express it, the charge dissipated and I was able to go beyond it to the next stages of resentment and shame.

Shame was big for me. For so long I felt my poor treatment was all my fault — if I was a better kid, if I was different, if I was good enough, then maybe I wouldn't have been treated that way.

I feel grateful for the awareness my inner work has brought. It is such a relief to know that there are reasons that I developed the way I did. It's not just craziness that I have certain issues to work on in my life. This work has allowed me glimpses into what I need to do to further heal myself. Also, I can now sometimes talk with friends, or read, or journal when it becomes confusing to try and determine what I want, rather than what someone else wants for me.

Q: It's truly a process isn't it? There is no one right way.

A: Yes. Every situation is different. I find it easier to fall back into the old patterns when I'm not in an optimal state — rested and feeling well. Right now I'm in a major transition in my life, having recently had a baby. Being very tired, I've found myself tending to want to repeat the old ways of letting others invade my boundaries. Fortunately, I'm more conscious of it now and I remind myself of my need to meditate, center, and get back on track.

Q: So in your case taking responsibility included being responsible for answering the question where do we go from here?

A: Yes. I don't want to drive my car by looking in the rearview mirror. I want the mirror there so I can look back and see what I need for a safe journey and to assist my ability to drive forward to where I want to go.

LOVE, DEPENDENCY, AND PROSPERITY

Your love belongs to you; you take it with you; you only share it.

Being prosperous is feeling fulfilled — "filled full" with a sense of life and love. In this state we are no longer searching for love, we are living love.

Ironically, to enjoy this emotional abundance, we must release our intense *need* for love — a major block to prosperity consciousness. As long as we stay in scarcity thinking we will never feel loved enough. When we feel needy, or deprived, our desire for love seems to outrun our supply.

Before discussing ways to avoid or release the repetitive cycle of scarcity thinking about love and relationships, let's look at how cultural training contributes to starting these cycles.

ACCEPTING THE ROLE

How have women allowed the need for love to supersede most other needs, drives, and desires?

It started very early, when we were petted, had our hair curled, told how sweet we were, and given dolls to play with. We got the message, and most of us liked it. As girls, our destiny was tied up with getting a boy to go with our playhouse.

We were groomed, and groomed ourselves, to catch a "love." Taking on characteristics of self-responsibility, independent thinking, and self-confidence was left to our brothers. Women are here to find someone to please. Men are here to provide, to be responsible, and to make us feel good about ourselves.

Without even knowing we were doing it, or what the rules of the game were — we bought this game. That's an important point to remember — that we did buy it, in different degrees and in different ways. There were benefits in accepting that receptive, pleasing role; we were to be provided for, taken care of. A bargain was made.

What we did, of course, was set up total dependence on the "great provider." Everything depended on the reaction of the male toward us. Our whole sense of rightness, of goodness as a person, of being of value to the world, depended upon a man's "love."

LOVE AND NEED

It is really hard to love someone you need. Without developing a strong inner-core feeling of independent strength, a centered awareness of self — separate from our partner — our "love" is more likely to be conditional. Most of us confuse love and need. Love is a spontaneous, pure outpouring of feeling, coming from within. Although we attribute others as being the "cause," real love toward others only comes when we have developed our capacity to feel love within.

Your love belongs to you; you take it with you wherever you go; you only share it. Love is self-generated — an extension of your inner being. There is no "bargain," no "exchange" in love. We love for love itself.

What we have called "love" in a relationship is very often a fulfilling of needs — a feeling of being grateful that we are being provided for, both in physical survival needs, and in emotional and psychological needs.

We limit our growth and potential experience when we confuse love with protecting and providing. Love then becomes the fulfillment of a role we have established. When we come together out of need, it can be to feed each other's weaknesses. For example, if you choose a partner because he can plug a hole that exists in your personality — for example, you're shy of meeting people so you (perhaps unconsciously) marry an assertive, outgoing partner who plays that role for you — then you never have to grow in that area.

Even in this new age when both women and men are taking time out to find who they are as people — separate from their roles — we still resist giving up the great myth. There must be some Shining Knight or Giant Mama who is going to save us from ourselves, to help us avoid learning what we need to learn in life, to validate us painlessly so we won't need to grow.

UNCONDITIONAL LOVE

What we are all looking for, of course, is that elusive unconditional, uncritical, and nonjudgmental love. What we all need to understand is simply: it starts within. When you let go of the judge and jury within, you will find a perennial garden of love.

PROSPERITY KEY NO. 5
We are all we need because we are what we desire.

You are already it. You are love; that is your true nature. Letting go of the great search for the perfect love, and looking within instead for your own reservoir of love can free up tremendous amounts of energy, which are then available for redirection.

As we begin to see the truth in this key, we also see that the female's compulsive desire for a providing, protective "love" is a deterrent to prosperity consciousness. Until we women come to understand to what extent we have been programmed to feel like women only when we are taken care of — when someone other than ourselves loves and accepts us — we will not even be free to desire true prosperity. That very concept will instead be threatening to our basic life structure built around the idea that women are first and foremost to be in the serving, giving role.

LOVE AS SERVICE

To many women, work is a filler — a "holding place" while we wait for life to begin. Many intelligent, creative, well-educated women devote years of their lives in voluntary or part-time, entry-level, low-paying jobs in order to carry out the image of themselves as servers.

In many cases, the jobs themselves are taken so we can do a double shift of serving and providing in our promotion of the well-being of others. Often, these jobs are attractive because they have the benefits of noncommitment and high mobility, and they are often short-term. All of this allows women to increase their support services but does little to promote the future career of the woman.

It is amazing how many young college women today are still not taking themselves seriously. They do not see themselves having a career, but rather see themselves "in English," or "in History" temporarily, until they get married. Although the trend is lessening, the college programs drawing the most women students are teaching, nursing, and secretarial. This still continues, in spite of the fact that the job market in teaching is at a low point, few secretaries make it up through the ranks into better-paying positions, and nurses as a rule feel underpaid for the tremendous amount of work and responsibility they have. None of these factors is deterring enrollment in these three areas.

As prospering women, we must recognize that even with twenty years out for raising a family, the average woman will work twenty to thirty years of her life. Realistically, for most of us, our life income and lifestyle are directly related to our job choice. Marriage no longer precludes working; half of all married women are working, often in low-paying clerical jobs. Even after ten years or more on such jobs, many of these women still picture themselves as "temporarily employed." Now, with half of our marriages ending in divorce, we see the added necessity of planning a work career with sufficient financial reward to support the family we are often left with.

For you to be prosperous, you will have to deliberately choose to be. You will have to reevaluate your life priorities, and take yourself, interests, and career seriously. You will have to look at your traditional role as server and giver to others, and decide what you want to give to yourself. In other words, you must reevaluate your "love priorities."

PROSPERITY KEY NO. 6
Love yourself first.

We have been taught from early childhood to "Love thy neighbor as thyself," and we have been given some idea of what "love thy neighbor" entails. But somehow the "love thyself" part has been sadly neglected — or worse, it has been given negative, narcissistic connotations. Many of my women clients have had difficulty even comprehending how to start to love themselves. I recommend a copy of this list be put up on the bathroom mirror, to be reviewed each day, for a healthy reminder of whom we must love first:

I Love Myself
I listen to what I want and I respond to that want.
I make my own rules to live by.
I give myself credit often.
I surround myself with beauty.
I create an abundance of friends.
I nourish myself with only good food.

I allow myself to have abundance in all ways.

I reward myself appropriately.

I trust myself.

I give myself pleasure in a variety of ways.

I enjoy the sensations of my body.

I enjoy sexuality.

I forgive myself.

I give myself authority.

I have fun.

I talk to myself gently.

I regard my needs, wants, goals, and welfare as important as anyone else's.

The beautiful lesson to be learned about love is that loving yourself does not take away from loving others. It is a prerequisite before genuine love can happen. Love only multiplies. You can only give that which you have. Unless you create love within, you have little to share with others.

LOVE, SEX, AND DEPENDENCY

A discussion of women and love and how they relate to prosperity is not complete without looking at the role sex plays as a driving, motivating, satisfying force for women. An interesting theory among some sex therapists is that women must have plenty of what is sometimes called "PSA" — pleasure, security, and approval — before they feel really fulfilled.

Trouble starts when we attempt to satisfy all three needs with our sexual relationships. Trying to meet security and approval needs through sex detracts from the pleasure sex naturally brings, and can make a stew out of our self-image. It sets up the possibility that we will feel insecure and disapproved of when we don't have a good, frequent sex life with a partner. When that happens, making love can become a desperate need for improving our self-esteem. Sex has then lost its value as a unique and separate experience. The experience of wanting to make love, versus desperately needing to make love to satisfy a suffering ego, are extreme opposites.

Feeling we have to wait for someone else to give us pleasure is yet another way we experience dependency. Prosperity is providing security and approval from within, not waiting for another to provide that security and approval.

As one sex counselor, Grace Darling, points out in her seminars on human sexuality, the female is complete in herself sexually. The female body is built for pleasure and she need never feel deprived. The clitoris is the only human organ whose sole function is giving pleasure. Women, therefore, do not need a man to experience sexual fulfillment. When we learn to separate the need for sexual satisfaction from the need for approval and security, we are free to be completely with a partner in a loving, giving way.

It is only when we learn that we can give ourselves pleasure, security, and approval that we then come from a centered place and can be totally with another without trying to figure out if we are loved enough. We experience true prosperity when we have already done that for ourselves!

On the Future

What's to come is a manifestation of my thoughts
What am I about?
Life is here to enjoy
I am life
I am not just here to do
This is a gift
I am also here to be.
Where I am present, I am going
When I am "present," I am giving.

PROSPERITY AND THE MIND

"There is nothing in the moving world but mind itself."
— Old Hindu Sutra

*H*ave you ever stopped to notice the overflowing abundance of nature and wondered if you too were born to prosper naturally? We have all we need at birth to develop into the miraculous mental and physical beings that we become as adults. Doesn't it make sense that, like the rest of nature, we would be equipped at birth with all the seeds necessary for our prosperous growth?

If prosperity is a natural condition, why does it seem so hard? Because, unlike the rest of nature, we humans must exercise choice in the development of our prosperity. To be human is to be self-aware with the ability to choose to develop a higher consciousness. Choice is the means and the end. Our growth — our prosperity — comes from our choice in the way we use our mind.

We are part of nature, but we are not blown by the wind and planted in the earth. We can decide where and when to plant our seeds. That is under our control. We can live a life being a victim, being dependent, responding automatically, or playing it safe in every way, and we may well survive. But if we want to plant those seeds of prosperity that we were all born with, we must deliberately choose to do so.

The source, or seed, of all prosperity is in the full use of our creative mind. By mind I mean more than brain. Our brain is only one small part of our mind. The mind refers to the information received from the *total self* — the mental, physical, emotional, and spiritual self. The extent to which we choose to listen to and act upon the information from this mind is the extent to which we will prosper.

Your thought, in the form of intuitive hunches, dreams, and gut reactions, is your connection with your total creative self. To help you act on the information given by your creative urges, you can begin by understanding the power of thought.

Here are four major points to consider when starting to use the power of creative thinking:

(1) *To develop your consciousness of prosperity, observe every day what you are creating with your thought.*

We first create in mental form everything we desire to produce in physical form. Look around you. Everything you see at this moment that is humanmade — whatever you wear, sit on, eat with, live in — was once only an idea in someone's mind. Think back over the last thing you created — a cake, a manuscript, a clean house, a painting, peace between two people — everything you do has the same beginning. It starts with a thought. It may happen so fast you don't notice it, but every move you make is preceded by a thought. We can literally say that we are our thoughts.

The power of thought is so incredible that it is awesome to try to describe. All physical reality that has been invented, discovered, or achieved by humans started as an idea. Every war or civic program had its origin in thought. We are totally surrounded and affected daily by the results of concentrated consciousness from hundreds of thousands of people whose minds came into agreement to produce our cultural accomplishments — bridges, buildings, systems of all sorts. Each project is physical proof of the power of collective thought.

Just having an idea, of course, is not enough to manifest it into material reality. Ninety percent of our ideas die upon conception, or soon afterward. At best, five percent survive long enough to become somewhat developed, and perhaps five percent see the light of day.

CONVINCE YOURSELF
AND YOU CONVINCE THE WORLD

Developed thought alone is not enough to manifest an idea into physical reality. It must be combined with belief. Unless you believe in your idea, it will die. Thought is the striking of the match, and belief is the keg of dynamite — the power behind the creative thought. Intention is the hand that strikes the match. You must know what you truly want — what your intention is — or you end up setting off kegs of dynamite in all directions as if they were firecrackers on the Fourth of July. Everybody enjoys firecrackers — but their effect is short-lived. Getting what you want out of life requires aligning thoughts, beliefs, and intentions.

What does this mean to us?

It means that no matter what has happened in our past, we are never helpless victims. We have the power to change, to be what we want to be, to have what we want to have. That power is our thought. When our thoughts are repeated often enough, they form a pattern. These thought patterns actually program our minds. Whatever we are programming our minds to create, they create.

(2) *For a thought to be generative, it must be sharply outlined or defined in the mind with a feeling of expectation.*

We tend to think about our wants in vague, undifferentiated, dreamlike states, without putting much mind energy behind them. That is because we find it difficult to believe that we can have what we want in life.

It's true wishful thinking has little power to manifest, but that isn't its purpose. A wish is like a spark — similar to the starter on an engine. You couldn't drive your car around the block using your starter, that's not what it's meant for. If you really wanted to read a book, would you try to do so with a match when you could light a candle? What we wish for, and what we expect, must be deliberately combined in order to create in reality a positive, prospering condition.

The real power behind manifestation lies in the state of expectation. Belief systems — our concepts about what makes life work — are the source of our expectations. Changing our expectations to align them more with what we want may require challenging our beliefs — something we don't do easily. The painful part about growing is that we must constantly challenge our beliefs. The pain comes from not wanting to let go of a position that has helped us get to wherever we are. Beliefs are a two-edged sword. They motivate us, keep us highly charged, keep us moving, and, at the same time, limit our access to other horizons.

Examples of limiting concepts I heard as a child include, "Life isn't a bed of roses, you know!" and "What you want and what you get are two different things." And they indicated to me that I should expect pain and misery in life, and not much of what I wanted.

Actually our whole concept of reality is limited until we experience the fact that the only reality there is is what we tell ourselves. What we believe, we become.

Because we act as if our beliefs are true, they have both positive and negative effects. When we perceive the world as a finished product with the rules and decisions already made, we walk around on egg shells, trying to fit into this world, fearful of disturbing the preexisting order. Wouldn't it be more fun to sense this world as a giant pile of raw lumber, just there for us to help create something better? This attitude would bring out the creative power we were born with. We want to allow our dreams to become clearer, and learn to expect to win, to really make a difference.

YOUR SUBCONSCIOUS POWER

(3) *In order to understand your creative, manifesting power, you need to differentiate between the roles of the conscious and the subconscious aspects of the mind.*

The conscious mind has the task of deciding what we want to create in our lives. It does this by sorting out our thoughts — judging and discriminating among them. Using past and present knowledge, plus all the input of the senses, it weighs evidence, makes priorities, and plans for the future. Best of all, it is under our control.

Not so the subconscious. Our knowledge of this aspect of mind is limited: we both fear and stand in awe of it. The subconscious was long ago acknowledged by psychologist Carl Jung and others as the power base of our being, the real source behind our creativity.

We are wary of being controlled by this power, especially when we feel pulled into actions that we do not consciously accept as beneficial. At those times it seems as if our deep-gut desires have taken over completely, ignoring our rational decisions. When that happens we feel controlled by the subconscious, yet almost helpless to stop it.

Harnessing the incredible power of the automatic machine, the subconscious, is what manifestation is all about. This task is one of the most exiting and rewarding challenges of our lives. Even at this moment our actions are being determined by this nucleus of energy — how wonderful if we could be in the driver's seat handling the reins!

HOW YOU CREATE

The subconscious mind is subjective in nature. This means that, unlike the conscious mind, it does not discriminate between thoughts. All are equally treated. All conscious thoughts that have penetrated the subconscious are accepted subjectively, without concern for their being right, wrong, good, or bad to the subconscious. If the conscious mind has said so, it is so.

Our subconscious mind is basically composed of "pictures" of all our conscious thought patterns developed over a lifetime. Any pattern of thought that is allowed to remain in our conscious mind long enough will eventually "sink into" our subconscious as a symbol representing those thoughts. All worries, fears, strongly felt desires, convictions, or beliefs that feel like they are a "part of us" are the thoughts we have kept around long enough to slip into our subconscious. When they do, they form a belief system stored in symbolic imagery. These images, which we have programmed in over the years, run our lives by unconsciously determining our actions and bring to us the positive or negative conditions they represent.

Change only comes when a newer thought with a stronger emotional impact "seeps through" from the conscious mind to counteract the first directive. In the meantime, the subconscious is moving the organism, robotlike, toward the programmed goal.

In this way, the subconscious is similar to an automatic pilot device that has been given coded messages about how to run a ship over the years, and is responding accordingly. All is well until the need of the ship's captain changes, and she finds the automatic device has rusted in place and no one knows how to reprogram it.

Whatever the conscious mind dwells upon becomes the orders for the subconscious to produce. The importance of realizing the subjective nature of the subconscious is to understand that the subconscious cannot say no. It is our impersonal genie who can only reply yes, totally accepting conscious thought as an absolute dictator.

That is both good news and bad news. The bad news is that because our culture, as most others, is so negative-prone, most of our programming has been influenced be negative thought — not only our own thoughts but all of those around us. From birth we have experienced daily a bombardment of negativity from parents, teachers, peers, fellow workers, and mates. Their intention is not negative; especially toward us, they are the result of their own negative programming too.

Nevertheless, the results are the same. It is all too easy for us to discuss in great detail what is wrong with us and others — what we can't do, what they did wrong, what we should have done, ways we ought to change, and why we can't. By clinging to our negative thoughts we have unwittingly allowed these attitudes to slip into the subconscious and dominate our creative energy.

Proof that our thought affects us, in both positive and negative ways, is easy to find. Faces, bodies, and actions of people around us reflect if they are happy, self-achieving, fulfilled people. When you are thinking joy, you are emanating joy all around you. Conversely, if your mind is absorbed with worry, doubt, and fear, that shows too. We attract or repel people according to our thoughts. When you think negatively, you turn away joy and love.

The good news is that we now have a chance to modify all this negativity in our lives. We can do it through deliberate, continuous, conscious canceling of negative thought and substituting positive patterns.

(4) *The thought most deeply impressed upon the subconscious creates what we manifest in our lives.*

It is our choice, and within our power, to deliberately select the thoughts we consciously hold.

By consciously repeating strongly desired thought goals for a sufficient amount of time, we are actually programming our subconscious to produce that goal. Once programmed, this great impersonal computer has no choice but to produce, without question, what we ask for, indefinitely.

This is where the role of the will plays its crucial part in manifesting. Many have mistakenly tried to use their will to push, shove, and force behavior to conform to their decisions of the ideal. The true role of the will is to be a guardian over our thoughts. Its task is to make sure that all our thoughts positively support our goals. By keeping negative thoughts out of the conscious mind, the will is being used on the highest level possible.

Sound like positive thinking? Yes, it is, but it is more. The head, heart, and gut work together. It is not enough to mouth the words about good in our lives, nor just to think the thought. We must seek it actively, feel it, and live it.

This is far from a Pollyanna approach to life. The negative cannot and should not be ignored. It is to be learned from. We need to not only acknowledge the negatives in our lives, but take responsibility for them, and see what we're getting out of them.

Resisting or hiding from pain may provide momentary pleasure, but it assures a lifetime of pain. Facing our problems may bring momentary pain, but brings a lifetime of pleasure. Working through negatives and living a negative life are two very separate things.

THE POWER OF CONSCIOUS THOUGHT

Because prosperity depends upon the full use of our creative imagination, we need to find ways to fully use the conscious mind. Our task, as of this moment, is to become aware of our own negative thoughts and deliberately cancel them with our willpower. Cleaning up our act from the inside means just that — staying with our own process and watching what we are telling ourselves.

To do this, we need to be constantly alert to the power of our thoughts, to know that there is no such thing as a casual statement.

Every time we make a statement we are reinforcing our future. Words are energy and energy is creative. As poet Ralph Waldo Emerson said, "Words are alive; cut them and they bleed." We will use this aliveness of our own words to create life and spirit for achieving our life goals. In order to creatively use the conscious mind to reprogram the subconscious, we will need to keep the conscious mind clear. We need to be able to (1) concentrate with clarity, (2) develop peace of mind, and (3) be present — *now*. Let's look at how we block the full use of our conscious mind through filtered consciousness, drifting consciousness, and the chattering mind.

FILTERED CONSCIOUSNESS

We often misunderstand the nature of the conscious mind and try to succeed by being a totally rational person. We strive to know "enough" to win in life. The conscious mind, however, is a gatherer.

The general public values information. Facts, figures, and hard data seem far more real to many people than intuitive guesses, prophetic dreams, or gut reactions. Yet, top leaders in every field easily recognize that many final decisions must often be based on information that goes beyond the facts. After the figures are gathered and digested, big decisions are usually made with intuitive leaps of the imagination. Many times we must ultimately decide with incomplete facts and instead rely on what feels right.

To stay more in touch with your intuitive feelings — the true source of prospering decisions — you need to go beyond interpreting your experiences through the filter of the conscious mind. Use it to classify, computerize, and decode information from the environment. Then *feel* the truth — be with nature and trust your gut reactions to people and problems.

DRIFTING CONSCIOUSNESS

Drifting consciousness is a way we have of disappearing mentally. When we are not present mentally, we are not available to all that is going on and we are not fully prepared to change if it becomes immediately necessary. Being here — now — is hard work, and absolutely necessary for prosperity consciousness. We must be present to act spontaneously, ready to take our next step when it shows itself.

So much of our time is spent in drifting consciousness, and in distraction, without even being aware of it. Each time we are driving down the road and suddenly "come to," not really certain where we are or where we've been, we can be sure we have been functioning on automatic pilot. We usually did not choose to reminisce, but instead were chasing an elusive thought that took us farther and farther away from being alive to the moment. Each time this happens we will want to gently refocus the mind on the present.

CHATTERING MIND

The third consciousness trap that prevents clarity of consciousness is the chattering mind. In its usual undisciplined state, the mind has been likened to a "drunken monkey," jumping about at random, going from one subject to another endlessly, producing little more than fatigue or, at best, escape. This is the opposite of the kind of directed attention necessary for prosperity consciousness. Prosperity demands concentrated thought. This idea is summed up in the following prosperity key.

PROSPERITY KEY NO. 7
Quieting the mind promotes directed action.

The incessant repetitive thoughts that obsess our minds are a drain on our creative energy. Are you aware of constantly talking to yourself? Take the next two minutes and write down all the thoughts that are going through your head. Note how unimportant most of them are, and how you repeat yourself. You probably won't be able to write fast enough.

Next, sit in front of a clock and try not to think for sixty seconds. Don't be discouraged by the results; you would have the powers of a very sophisticated yogi if you could stop your mind for just three minutes. Fortunately, you don't need to be a yogi to reap the benefits of quieting your mind.

A simple and effective way to stop the chatter in your head is to say "Stop!" to yourself when you hear your "reverberating circuits" going around endlessly. An even more effective, longer-lasting technique is to meditate. If you are a beginner, take fifteen minutes each morning, close your eyes, breathe deeply, relax your body, and when thoughts come, just announce to yourself, lovingly, "Peace. Be still." Meditation is a form of acknowledging your connection with the spirit of universal love, and it allows for a sense of peace and love to flood your being. The tranquillity that follows stays with you, reducing stress and promoting a state of creative awareness throughout the day.

Many artists have spoken of the creative state of being they achieve by quieting the mind and focusing attention through meditation. Just sitting quietly gives you a chance to go inside to ask your most important questions to your inner self. German composer and pianist Johannes Brahms, for example, wrote about his feeling of being a channel of creative energy during meditation:

I always contemplate my oneness with the creator before commencing to compose. This is the first step. I immediately feel vibrations that thrill my whole being. These are the spirit illuminating the soul power within and in the exalted state I see clearly what is obscure in my ordinary moods; then I feel capable of drawing inspiration from above ... straight-away the ideas flow in upon me and not only do I see distinct themes in my mind's eye, but they are clothed in the right forms, harmony, and orchestration. Measure by measure the finished product is revealed to me when I am in those rare inspired moods.

Creative energy is waiting to move through us once we get out of our own way. Cleansing the mind of negative thought, quieting the chatter, and becoming one with the moment provides the environment for this energy to flow freely through us.

PROSPERITY PROFILE NO. 7

Interview with Gudrun Höy, leading-edge educator, consultant, lecturer, and seminar leader who founded and directed the Children's Circle Center in Tiburon, California, a model school in Marin County for multicultural, global education. She is presently the educational director for Enchanté, a multimedia company dedicated to bringing the concept of "emotional literacy" to parents, educators, and children all over the country.

Q: There is a feeling of such joy in your school for children — tell me how did you go from seed thought to manifesting this dream?

A: I'm a first generation immigrant. I came on my own from Denmark when I was eighteen to spend six months as an *au pair* for a family in Orinda. I was planning to be a teacher in Early Childhood Education in Denmark, but I felt so inspired by my experiences here that after returning to Denmark, I knew I had to come back.

I lived in Berkeley in the late 1960s and knew little about the context in which I found myself. I was completely and totally naive — which I think helped me to survive a couple of unusual situations. But I did get a tremendous sense of energy from the social consciousness and the revolutions that were going on. For a young person, I found that extremely exciting.

I've been in the United States twenty-five years. I received my education here. All through the years, I've always been outspoken about how I think early childhood education should be changed, and eighteen years ago friends of mine, educators and philanthropists who are independently wealthy, came to me and said, "We think you should start your own school. You always seem to have so many ideas, why don't you do your own thing." I was twenty-seven and just out of my second marriage. My personal life was in chaos but I felt driven in my work. I knew I was green behind the ears, but something inside me said, "You'd better go with this. There is something here that I know, strongly, from somewhere, and I think I can make this happen."

They encouraged and financially supported the project for the first three to four years. I had to decide where I wanted the school to be and what the emphasis was going to be on. I decided on Marin because of the possible association with the local college. I did a needs assessment and got the necessary license and found an old mansion to make into a warm environment for the children. The rooms were beautiful, all painted in primary colors. We had fish tanks built into the shelves so the light would come through them, and plants everywhere.

It was beautiful. I put together my philosophy of the program, hired the people, and we started in June 1976, with one paid student, two others I had invited to keep that student company, and three very anxious teachers. By the end of the summer we had twenty-four children. The school has been going on its own since.

The one thing that has amazed me was how much I intuitively knew about education in that early, idealistic phase of my life. By some miracle, I really did know from somewhere, and the philosophy I set out with has been consistent all these seventeen years of the evolution of this school. The school has become my lab for all I have been through, as a woman, as an educator, and as a parent.

Q: Tell me about your vision.

A: Visions are tough because by their very nature they are very ideal-istic. The vision I have is based on my belief that every child deserves to be respected and honored for what he or she is — a unique human being in all his or her developmental areas. Each area is equally important. We often think of education as an academic pursuit, but it's not. It's about the social, physical, personal, and creative develop-ment of the child. My philosophy spills over into my work at Enchan-té, whose emotional literacy campaign is dedicated to producing materials — books, audiotapes, and television programs — specifical-ly to teach children about their emotional development.

Q: The creative development is most often overlooked. Too often it is considered only if there is money left over.

A: Yes, and most often there isn't. It's considered a luxury, yet it is the very essence of humanity and of civilization.

We need to instill in the child a respect for life, to provide an environment where trust can develop and where the child will feel safe as he or she unfolds. Education does not stop with learning to read and write. We need to help our children shape an attitude about life at an early stage. We need to teach them that we live in a multi-cultural, global world, and we need to support children becoming global citizens.

I've worked hard to have the children be surrounded by people who share the philosophy of needing to think globally, but the actual doing of it is a process. The effects may not show up in learning curves, or text scores, but it's an intrinsic part of what's happening here.

It has become a place of women. One good thing that happens when we come together as a staff is that there is a tremendous amount of support among us while still being very professional.

We're here to teach. Yet the vision is not just for the children. The vision is for everyone — for the people who work here and for the parents that come in here. The modeling that we do needs to be shared by all.

Q: I imagine you've had some wonderful success stories.

A: One child comes to mind — an East Indian child from a very difficult background of divorced parents. He could not read or write, he couldn't even show his face. Most of the time his face was down and his shoulders were up. He was growing his hair as long as he possibly could. He wanted to hide from life. What happened for this child was that in two years he saw himself as a leader. We got to see his beautiful face, and he learned to read and write — extremely well. He even became our computer expert. We tried to work with the family, but had to be content with getting some therapy for the boy. He went out of here feeling capable, knowing that he was somebody! As a teacher, if you know you've succeeded with even *one* student, that's enough reward; you have it made.

Q: *Prospering Woman* is really about following your inner guidance, and that is what I hear in your story, that you have trusted and followed this guidance to find yourself and your true work.

A: I am a spiritual person, not a religious one, but once you recognize the feeling of being guided within yourself, you can give into that, and you don't need to argue against it.

Clearly, in my work I feel guided. The danger when you have a strong vision is your ego. I have had to learn to drop the ego part and know that the more I can be a tool to do what I do best, the more fulfilling it is for me. On the other hand, if you are too modest, that can be ego also. You can be your own worst enemy through the limitations of doubts and fears.

Q: What do you believe has helped you the most to manifest your dreams into reality?

A: I am even more passionate about my work now than when I first became interested at age sixteen. But I have learned to see things at arm's length. I've learned not to take everything personally.

Also, I've always been a team player. My vision doesn't make me any better than anybody else. Many people do important work for the school. I've been given a gift — a spark of interest in something that inspires me, and I have been able to nurture that gift. If I can inspire one other person, or help to bring about change in one of the areas I feel so strongly about, I will feel even more fulfilled.

One of the most important things I've learned has been to recognize when to let go. This means learning how and when to bring other people into the vision early enough in the process so they become co-owners. It's about empowering other people so they feel they have a very important piece of the work. It's delegating, actually — to give choices, and then let go, let go, let go. Not let go of the vision, for that does not have to be compromised, but to let go of the need to control.

9

PROSPERITY CONSCIOUSNESS

"Our life always expresses the result of our dominant thoughts."
— Soren Kierkegaard

*P*rosperity requires that we know and follow the laws of prosperity.

We already know the profound effect that the discovery of physical laws has had on the development of modern life. The discoveries making civilization possible were as available to Neanderthal humans as they are to us. Stone Age minds, however, were not ready to observe, understand, or apply the information available. The difference between then and now is primarily in the development of consciousness. It is this same growth in awareness that is now leading us to want to know the laws of mental manifestation.

Part Two introduces the laws of prosperity, which are tools to help you produce in physical form what you desire. These laws show you ways of releasing the potential of your creative mind. This creative mind is the sum total of information from your physical, mental, emotional, and spiritual self. It is the source within you that unites you with the energy of the universe.

To fully utilize the laws of prosperity, you will want to view them as laws of consciousness. By changing our attitude through belief, expectation, and acceptance, we are really describing a change of consciousness about the so-called "real world."

What is real to you?

Most people will bang the table and say, "That's real! It's solid!" We can feel, taste, touch, smell it. But how solid is solid? Modern science has told us that in spite of how it appears, all mass is actually atomic particles in constant motion. These particles are vibrating and circulating with intense speed, reacting with each other in ceaseless, complex patterns. In breaking these whirling atoms down to their smallest dimension, scientists have found to their amazement that ultimately there are no building blocks of mass — there is only energy. Physicist Fritjof Capra, speaking on the nature of matter in *The Tao of Physics*, said:

> The discovery that mass is nothing but a form of energy has forced us to modify our concept of a particle in an essential way. In modern physics, mass is no longer associated with a material substance, and hence particles are not seen as consisting of any basic "stuff," but as bundles of energy.

MANIFESTING ENERGY

The process of manifestation involves working with mental energy in such a way that mind has control over matter. If the reality of all mass, or matter, is that it is only energy, we need to learn to work with energy to create a life of abundance. What can we deduce about the nature of this energy?

From astronomy and physics we know that all life, all matter, exists within the context of an infinite universe. Infinite is often defined as "having no limit in power, capacity, and knowledge; extending indefinitely; inconceivably great; inexhaustible." If our infinite universe consists only of energy, then this energy, too, has to be infinite — powerful, beyond limit.

Understanding the interrelationship between infinite energy and the power of the mind to create form is the most challenging and rewarding investigative study of this century. It will be through this study that we may eventually be able to know how the mind manifests. As of now, we can only observe that it indeed does, and make conjectures about how it does.

We have never had large-scale, government-supported research in parapsychology, the study of the mind, such as that found in other countries — especially Russia. This is due primarily to the lack of interest by science as a whole, and the lack of funds to support the effort. Individuals from various disciplines, including Nobel laureates in the fields of physics, psychology, philosophy, and metaphysics, however, have been fascinated be the powers of the mind.

Psychologists, philosophers, and other great minds of the past, including William James, Albert Einstein, Luther Burbank, Thomas Edison, and Carl Jung, have all actively engaged in some form of study of psychic interaction with matter. According to author Marilyn Ferguson in *The Aquarian Conspiracy*, generally, as these great minds studied these interactions, they went through "a chronology of interest: first fascination, fear, or both; then avoidance of the phenomena as a distraction . . . and, finally, acceptance of them as natural, plausible, and an extension of human creative powers, and evidence of the essential unity of all life."

The Aquarian Conspiracy is an excellent resource of information on current serious, scientific inquiry into all aspects of the mind — biofeedback, extrasensory perception, intuition, right- and left-brain hemisphere differences, mind transference, and other creative powers. We are able to study some mind-matter interactions in a laboratory setting, but, as yet, much of the research being done on how the mind moves matter has proven somewhat inconclusive. Some of the research she reports, is highly exciting, however. For example:

Human intention has been shown to interact with matter at a distance, affecting the particles in a cloud chamber, crystals, and the rate of radioactive decay.

An intention to heal has been demonstrated to alter enzymes, hemoglobin values, and the hydrogen-oxygen bond in water. . . .

Says Ferguson, scientists admit that "every human intention that results in physical action is, in effect, mind over matter." Beyond individual, isolated, scientific experiments, one of the greatest boosts for the promotion of serious research on the power of the mind comes from the new quantum physics. Under the old Newtonian physics, it was thought that we lived in a mechanistic world which ran like a machine, with precise, predetermined clockwork action. Once it was proven that the act of observing changes that which is observed, we needed a new theory to explain reality.

Quantum physics provides for the phenomenon of mind affecting matter. In this new physics, the universe is seen as a dynamic whole which always includes the observer in an essential way. It is a discipline that allows in mathematical language for the unpredictable — the effect on matter of the observing consciousness.

MATTER, TIME, SPACE, AND ONENESS

Since manifesting involves the movement of matter through time and space, we need to look for a moment at what we know about the interrelationships between these elements. In our universe, infinite energy takes the form of visible and invisible matter. Matter has form and exists in space.

We also know that space and matter are both required for time to exist. Time is defined as that period required for one body to pass from one point to another. Without points of reference (that is, matter), therefore, there can be no time. When there is no space, there is no concept of distance, or of being separate. When there is no time or space, everything exists now, always and everywhere — infinitely.

INFINITE ONENESS

What does all this mean for manifesting with mind power? We have known for some time that energy and matter are interchangeable. Nothing is ever lost or gained; it is only converted. Therefore, when we see that matter is, in physics, equivalent to energy, we begin to understand the infinite unity of space, matter, and mind.

We are truly united in a conscious spirit that cannot be destroyed. We are at one with the universe. Wherever a part of this unity is, the whole is. Wherever we are, the universe is.

Therefore, at the energy level, that which we desire is already ours. According to Fritjof Capra:

The basic oneness of the universe is ... one of the most important revelations of modern physics.

In ordinary life, we are not aware of this unity of all things, but divide the world into separate objects and events. This division is, of course, useful and necessary to cope with our everyday environment, but it is not a fundamental feature of reality.

Some metaphysicians, in their study of the basic oneness of mind and matter, have looked at everything we have manifested and have observed that mental intention has influenced matter. Looking for cause and effect, they feel we are in error if we give credit, exclusively, to the rational mind for these creative advancements. Rational thought, they say, is only the channel or connection with our real creative source, the subconscious.

Thomas Troward, metaphysician, scholar, and close friend of philosopher William James, felt that the nature of infinite energy is so much like the nature of our subconscious mind that they must be closely connected. He saw this connection as the magic key to the source of the powerful creative forces of the mind.

Troward observed that both infinite energy and the subconscious mind are subjective in nature. This means that they are both acted upon and never instigate action:

1. Neither has the power of decision making, so neither can choose to respond from persuasion or from a sense of right or wrong.
2. Neither operates from a personal preference — helping some and deliberately hurting others.
3. They both operate purely from cause and effect. In other words, all things being the same, a specific cause will always produce the same specific result.
4. They are both material from which other things are formed.

His conclusion then is that our subconscious mind represents a small part of the universal mind or infinite energy. *Our subconscious mind would therefore be our connection, our access, to the unlimited resources of the universe.*

As we recognize our oneness with all there is, we sense what is possible when we concentrate our energy on any one desired result. If we are one, then we are not separate from that which we desire; it is already ours in thought form. It is our creative thought power that brings it into physical form, because it is our thought energy in the subconscious that unites us with the subjective infinite energy.

By its very nature, the power of infinite energy has to be drawing upon the energies of everything from everywhere at all times. By willfully choosing to allow only positive thought patterns to remain in our conscious minds, we are programming our subconscious to tune into this unlimited storehouse of infinite energy.

BRINGING THIS DOWN TO EARTH

For so long we women have grown up thinking that if we were lucky we would find someone who would somehow tell us how to live. Some expert would give us the magical word on what we wanted, and on how to get it. We have thought we must plead for help either because we were helpless, or because we were worthy and deserved help.

Yet, it seems safe to assume that any laws governing infinite energy must be universal by nature, working without exception for all alike. This energy can only work within its subjective powers; making exceptions is beyond its scope, against its very nature. It follows, then, that it would be inappropriate for you to work with infinite energy with the attitude of needing to coax or persuade the universe because you're worthy or needy.

This new approach suggests to you that you already have all you need within — that you are, naturally, connected with universal energy, which is all there is. Your job, then, is to fully open your own channel, your own connection with this energy, knowing you already deserve a fully rewarding life, and have everything you need to create it.

Part Two:

Receiving

*G*etting what we want out of life requires that we be ready to receive what is naturally ours. Until now, we have focused on clearing the mind of attitudes that keep us from prosperity or our missions in life. We are now ready to open the mind to its highest potential — as a channel of connection with our three selves: the lower (subconscious) mind, the conscious mind, and the higher universal mind.

In Part Two, we learn how to put more of our potential to work with a "concentrated mind action" process. The basic ideas of this process are not new — they are based on ancient truths. The truly successful have found and used portions of this path to prosperity throughout the ages.

I have combined these prosperity laws in a step-by-step process that allows you to readily assimilate and apply them to everyday situations.

CONCENTRATED MIND ACTION
NINE STEPS TO PROSPERITY

Get Ready:

Step 1 — Prosperity Law No. 1, The Law of Self-Awareness: We can only have what we want when we know who we are and what we want.

Step 2 — Prosperity Law No. 2, The Law of Wanting: Experiencing choice means knowing what we want and why we want it. Only then do we have the excitement and energy to go after our desires.

Step 3 — Prosperity Law No. 3, The Law of Planning: Without planning there is no consistent prosperity.

Get Set:

Step 4 — Prosperity Law No. 4, The Law of Releasing: We must get rid of what we don't want to make room for what we do want.

Step 5 — Prosperity Law No. 5, The Law of Compensation: There is a price for everything and we always pay.

Go:

Step 6 — Prosperity Law No. 6, The Law of Attraction: We attract what we are.

Step 7 — Prosperity Law No. 7, The Law of Visualization: We become what we imagine, positive or negative.

Step 8 — Prosperity Law No. 8, The Law of Affirmation: We become what we want to be by affirming and acting on our belief that we already are there.

Step 9 — Prosperity Law No. 9, The Law of Loving: Whatever goodness we want for ourselves we must also desire for others.

Each step is built upon the results of the previous step. We experience true prosperity when all the laws are followed. For this reason, read through the next nine chapters, then go back and start working on one step at a time. Incorporate the ideas your inner awareness has revealed to you in the process of reading these laws. Don't expect to do everything all at once, or you may feel overwhelmed and give up. It is important to both see the whole process and to attempt just one step at a time.

SELF-AWARENESS:
WHO AM I?

*Our essence does not have a need for material
possessions to be satisfied. It is complete in itself.*

PROSPERITY LAW NO. 1:
THE LAW OF SELF-AWARENESS

**We can only have what we want when we
know who we are and what we want.**

Did you ever, as a child, look in a mirror or sit on the side of a
pool of water and look at your own reflection and wonder,
Who am I? I remember one day standing in front of a three-way mirror in a neighbor's house when I was thirteen. I was fascinated that I
could see so many sides of me by moving one mirror — or both. I
looked so different depending on the angle.

My need to look at different aspects of myself didn't stop in ado-
lescence. I soon found that what I wanted in life depended on how I
defined myself. How I defined myself depended on how I looked at
myself. A good example of this was my going through a period in

which I thought I had to define myself as a "strong" woman or a "weak" woman.

Finding the answers to Who am I? and What do I want? is the hardest part in life. Getting what we want is a cinch after that — it's all downhill. Learning who the "I" is in the question Who Am I? is what this chapter is all about.

The following approach to understanding yourself can be used at any age. With repetition, this approach helps you keep a running profile on how you see yourself. We will look for the "I" through our subpersonalities versus the inner-self, and through ego versus essence.

SUBPERSONALITIES

One theory of personality, psychosynthesis, indicates that we are not one "I," but rather a complex group of "I"s — a collection of subpersonalities.

Subpersonalities are different sides of us that have developed as a result of our interaction with the world in different capacities. As our roles, interests, and moods change, the way we respond to the environment changes. We are much different with our bosses, for example, than we are with our mothers. We do not usually act the same with all our friends either. Every person brings out different aspects of us. In other words, the way we dress, act, and think can change quite dramatically depending on the people we're with and the situations we're in.

Can you think of ways you are different with different people? Roles call for various responses from us and we play dozens of roles. What are some of the roles in your life — sweetheart, wife, mother, cook, sister, secretary, president? What position toward the world do you take in each role? What makes you happy in each role?

Other subpersonalities develop around dominant attitudes, moods, and feelings. For example, the "Happy Helper" is continuously there to please, and will bend over backward to help anybody, anywhere, anytime. The "Pessimist" remains so in the best of situations. The "Judge" always has an improvement that could be made. If one subpersonality is strong enough, it can dominate — no matter what role is being played.

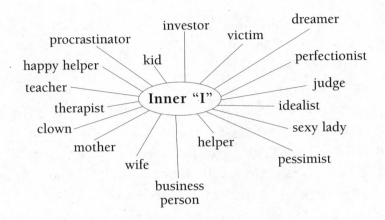

Subpersonalities are complex ways in which we interact with others. They often pass for being the real "I."

We all have a dozen or more subpersonalities and are usually operating in two or three at any given time. Each subpersonality wants something from us, and is offering something to us — all at once! In order to find peace and satisfaction in life, we need to identify our subpersonalities and discover what each one wants from us. Here's how:

1. Ask yourself the question "Who Am I?" twenty or thirty times. Write down your answers. Many of the attitudes, feelings, interests, and ideas about yourself will emerge.
2. Categorize your answers by themes. In what way do your answers seem to be connected with each other? (For example, some of my answers had to do with my concern for family, profession, health, love, security, fun, and strong feeling states.)

3. Give your subpersonalities a name, and picture them in your mind.
4. List what each subpersonality wants in life. Do any of these wants conflict? When our subpersonalities have opposing wants, we feel as if there is a war going on inside us. We often end up in confusion over our goals because of this disparity.

For example, Martha, an older client of mine, had entered college after twenty years of devoting herself to being a wife and mother, and was experiencing some deep inner turmoil by her changing desires. She came to therapy in great confusion and had to uncover the sabotage being caused by her different subpersonalities. One part of her, "Student Martha" was now making great demands on her time. But "Child Martha" was getting pouty because she wanted more time to relax and enjoy life. Child Martha undercut Student Martha's efforts at every opportunity. To complicate matters, "Judge Martha" was always there — usually with derisive statements about responsibility to the family.

"Wife Martha," trying to play her multiple roles such as "Sensuous Lady" and "Ms. Efficiency," was feeling stressful from lack of time and energy. "Mother Martha" was seeing her cherished role diminished (the children were now grown), and she experienced this as a great sense of loss.

"Banker Martha" was constantly warning that less time should be spent on schooling for the future and more time spent on earning money now. As these and other subpersonality voices were speaking nearly simultaneously, and each was demanding a great deal of attention, few needs were actually being met.

The value in identifying her subpersonalities in this manner was that Martha was able to stop blaming others for her anxiety, conflict, and pain and see clearly that the real source of her upsets was inside herself. Her change in values and shift in priorities required some internal dialogue among her conflicting subpersonalities.

By setting up a circle of chairs and pretending to speak as each subpersonality, she was able to listen to what each wanted and to hear what each was contributing to her life. She then saw how she could compromise and give a little time to each and bring balance internally. The outside world was easy after that.

The object of looking at subpersonalities is not to become schizoid by seeing all the opposing parts, but to improve our ability as a conductor in charge of this orchestra of virtuosos. We become victimized by putting too much energy into any one aspect of ourselves and overidentifying with any one part to the exclusion of others.

While subpersonalities do not need all they are demanding, if any one of them should feel starved for attention, she can become a real nuisance. Did you ever just have to go out for a candy bar or ice cream cone at midnight after a long, exhausting day? That's the child in you. Children will only be put off so long. With too many undernourished parts, we have a rebellion on our hands. Our peace is quickly gone, and our sense of prosperity has moved farther away.

We need to bring balance to the demands of our subpersonalities, allowing ourselves to move forward toward a chosen goal. See the parts of yourself as an impartial observer would. Ask each part what she wants, and what she is providing to your life. Prioritize their needs. Work toward a balance in meeting those needs by allotting some time and energy for each part. To get what you want in life with the minimum amount of inner opposition, make sure your major wants are satisfying the majority of your subpersonality needs.

INNER SELF

We developed each subpersonality as a way of expressing ourselves in the world. They are a reflection of our responses to environmental needs which are always changing. Another part of our "I-ness" is unrelated to changing circumstances. This is our central "I" or "inner self" behind our subpersonalities. This "I" is always quiet, always centered. As you still your chattering mind, you feel its calm, "knowing" strength that speaks when you're ready to listen. Another way of looking at this inner "I" is to see it as expressing your essence.

EGO VERSUS ESSENCE

The ego "I" is who we think we are. We created it, and by its very nature it is limited. When we are in ego, we constantly judge and compare ourselves with others. We feel separate from, out of touch with, our oneness with the universe. We rarely feel satisfied, for the ego is greedy and there is never enough to feel full. In ego consciousness, our real wants are often hidden from us.

If ego is who we *think* we are, then essence is who we *really* are. Essence is our true nature, that part of us that has never changed, is never fearful, never lost. The spirit of essence is like a tiny flame, mostly forgotten, but still determined to be.

Breathing life into this aspect of ourselves, we recognize that essence is our "light" within — that soft voice of inner awareness that connects us with all there is. In this state of mind, we see we are a child of the universe, that we already are a miracle. When we are in touch with our essence, we do not have to prove anything to anyone, nor get permission or approval from anyone in order to be ourselves.

Our essence does not have a need for material possessions to be satisfied. It is complete in itself. In seeking to satisfy our essence, we are seeking our highest good.

By limiting ourselves just to satisfying ego wants, we can become exhausted. Satisfying our essence can balance us and nourish us at a deep level. Anytime we express who we truly are, we are satisfying essence.

Give yourself plenty of quiet time alone with nothing to do in order to get in touch with essence. By acknowledging essence, our real "I," we feel closer to our spiritual nature. In this consciousness we know as long as our desires are life-affirming, and for the good of all, we deserve what we desire. With this freeing, prospering consciousness, we can go after what we want with a lighter heart, unattached to results.

This allows us to handle another paradox in prospering: We need to want with a strong desire and at the same time let go of attachment to a particular outcome. Coming from our essence, we know our good fortune does not depend upon any one outcome. We begin to trust the universal mind — the source of all prosperity.

Finding our peace, our center, our true "I," is not always easy. We have layer upon layer of conflicting shoulds and can'ts covering that little flame and the wisdom it imparts. It can be reached, however, by a variety of paths, some of which are deliberate, such as yoga, breath work, body work, therapy, dream work, and meditation.

Our centered "I" is also sometimes reached in the most unexpected ways, such as quietly walking on the beach, making love, jogging, looking at the clouds. At such moments, we can temporarily transcend our ego, making possible that high moment of contact with our essence, where we know that everything is perfect in the universe, here and now.

To feel fully satisfied by our efforts, our wants must be based on an awareness of who that "I" is that we're trying to satisfy — at the subpersonality and ego level, and at the level of essence. Only then can we best utilize our time and energy to get the most out of life. Finding out who we are is an exciting ongoing process. To start with, reflect on these words of wisdom handed down through the centuries telling us who we are:

> We are not our feelings and emotions —
>   although we have feelings and emotions.
> We are not our bodies —
>   although we have bodies.
> We are not our minds —
>   although we have minds.
> We are a center of consciousness —
>   wisdom, truth, and power.

11

WHAT DO I WANT?
THE FEELING RESPONSE

Powerful, impelling goals have the full force
of the self emerging from bondage.

PROSPERITY LAW NO. 2:
THE LAW OF WANTING

Experiencing choice means knowing what we want
and why we want it. Only then do we have the
excitement and energy to go after our desires.

*D*enise was a grad student and she was in love. More than anything, she wanted to have a reprieve from her master's program and go to Tahiti with her boyfriend and his parents over spring
break. They were leaving in three months, and it would cost her one
thousand dollars to go. She was a full-time student, didn't have a job,
and had only a few hundred dollars in her checking account.

When she asked my advice, I suggested she write a letter to the
universe, stating exactly what she wanted, and how she wanted to
receive it. She wrote the following letter:

Dear Universe,

Please send me $1,000 by June 1st. I need the deposit of $400 by May 1st to go to Tahiti. I really want to go. I want to work in the afternoons at $5.00 an hour doing something that I enjoy. I want to be able to study on the job, too. Thank you.

Love,

Denise

Impossible? Maybe. Improbable? Surely. Yet, within twenty-four hours Denise had a baby-sitting job at $5.00 an hour, taking care of a two-year-old boy. His parents, both professionals, were willing to pay a slightly higher hourly rate than they had budgeted simply for Denise's enthusiasm and love for their son. Denise could also study during his nap time.

As the money accumulated, Denise paid her deposit on May 1, and saw she would have the balance due in June. She was concerned about telling the mother she was quitting; she knew the family depended on her. When it came time to mention that next week would be her last, the mother interrupted her by saying she was pregnant and had decided to stay home after one week!

Denise's dream came true because she learned how to use the prosperity law of wanting. She dreamed the impossible and believed she could have it. Her experience gave her what many of us want — the feeling we can do or be whatever we want. Prosperity, as she found out, is the result of deliberate wanting and planning. Our ability to want is a magical gift. When we are excited and motivated to want, we are experiencing a sense of aliveness, and an inner awareness of unlimited opportunities about us. Planning puts a structure around that excitement to take us where we want to go.

IT'S OKAY TO WANT

We must give ourselves permission to desire what we want. We are created to want; it's natural. Wanting is how we grow. We are not selfish, bad, or greedy when we want — we are stretching to realize more of our potential.

At first glance this may appear to be the opposite of the Zen approach to self-fulfillment and peace of mind, which says the answer is to desire less. However, even those studying Zen are still intently desiring peace of mind. Ralph Waldo Emerson once remarked:

> The philosophers have laid the greatness of man in making his wants few, but will a man content himself with a hut and a handful of dried peas? He is born to be rich.... Wealth requires — besides the crust of bread and the roof — the freedom of the city, the freedom of the earth, traveling, machinery, the benefits of science, and fine arts, the best culture and the best company. He is the rich man who can avail himself of all men's faculties.

Fortunately, more women are availing themselves of the good things in life by giving themselves permission to desire better jobs, better pay, better health, more equal relationships, more satisfying sex. The world is feeling the effect of those desires, and as a result we are experiencing faster change than in any other peaceful revolution in the recorded history of womankind.

THE POWER OF WANTING

Wants are thoughts, and thought — as mind energy — is creative power. When we become specific about what we want, we are focusing the power of thought on our desires. Focusing attention intensifies energy in the same way a magnifying glass held over kindling will intensify the sun's power to start a fire. The more specific we are about our goals, the more intensely conscious we become about reaching them, and the greater the force of manifestation we create.

Studies have shown, however, that most of us have not formulated precisely what we want. Less than three percent of us have written out our goals. Our wants appear nebulous and difficult to put a finger on. It seems easier to live with the vague sense that something is missing, and to make do, rather than define what that something is. Late American psychologist Leon Festinger, who is best known for his cognitive dissonance research, has shown that when we get what we don't want, we soon start perceiving it as what we do want so we are not miserable! There's no way to know our real wants when we pretend we've got what we want.

BARRIERS TO WANTING

Why is it that we have so much reluctance to state specifically what we want in life?

There are a variety of reasons, but the root cause seems to be fear of failure. If we state what we want, then we're admitting we don't have it — and that feels like failing before we start. Other fears are:

"If I say what I want, and I don't get it, others will know it and I'll be embarrassed...."

"What's the use of deciding? I won't get it anyway."

"If I go for what I want and I get it, if I don't like it, I'm stuck with it."

We can release these negative thoughts of failure once we understand the beneficial role of failing. Failure is part of the package of learning. When a baby is learning to walk, she falls. We wouldn't think of condemning her for falling. So, too, when we are learning to want, and to establish goals based on those wants, we need to keep our focus on success. Our goals are not set in concrete — they can always change. When our desires turn out to be not so desirous, we can discard them and try again. Successful people know the importance of remaining flexible and of keeping their goals reflective of their feelings. They never lose sight of what they want, but when their plans fall through, they haven't failed. There is always more than one way to do anything we want to do. There's no such thing as failure anyway — there is only result. When we try a different approach, we get a different result.

Another major reason we have difficulty knowing what we want in life is that we have diluted our wants with shoulds. As a child, when we knew what we wanted and said so, Mom and Dad and others often told us that we "really didn't want it, now did we?" We nodded our heads, and guessed we didn't. And something happened.

We learned to stop wanting. Since then, the whole structure of society has eagerly taken over where Mom, Dad, and the educational institutions stopped. We were told in school what was good for us, and therefore what to desire. Our entire commercial advertising and merchandising system feeds on developing and directing our wants. Under these pressures, we forgot how to think through wants for ourselves.

Defining our desires specifically sometimes seems to be an overwhelming task. One friend recently felt she would have to give up everything she was presently doing — quit her job, leave her marriage, leave town — before she could know what she wanted. This was too scary for her, so she did nothing.

One way out of this dilemma is to ask your inner awareness to guide you in your goal-setting task. Ask yourself, "What is my next step?" A step is not a leap. By taking one step at a time, we can try some things out, and feel if our goal is right.

GOALS AND VALUES

Do your goals reflect your values?

As we learn to utilize goal setting to create desirable changes, we need to acknowledge our values. Wants which nourish are built on values we hold dear. These values, through our belief systems, are unconsciously determining our behavior patterns at every moment. Yet, few people can identify their values. Do you know what is important to you?

Look over the following quiz and let these questions stimulate your psyche to think about values that are real for you. The origin of your values has long been unconscious, but just answering a few simple questions will quickly reveal personal preferences. Sharing answers with a friend is very helpful too, especially as you bring out details in your discussion.

Values — being self-reliant, daring, logical, loving, polite, tidy, congruent, truthful, honest, capable, forgiving, responsible, self-controlled, open-minded, and so on — are only implied in our answers. We must look between the lines. Our values emerge in our choice of work, how we relate to people, how we spend our time, how we spend our money — everything we say, do, and think.

VALUES QUIZ

1. Answer these questions off the top of your head:

   If you had only three years to live, how would you structure your
      life?
   What three things do you want people to remember about you?
   How would you finish the sentence: "Happiness is. . . ."
   What two events in your life are you the most proud of?
   What always makes you angry?

2. What is important to you in your personal relations and life experiences? Rate these items on a scale of 1 to 10 (1 having a very low value to you, 10 being highly valued) and share with a friend why each is important:

A loving relationship _____
Being physically attractive _____
A satisfying marriage _____
Two months' vacation a year _____
A chance to be creative _____
Making a difference in the world _____
Freedom to make your own decisions _____
A beautiful home _____
Optimal health _____
Unlimited travel _____
Honesty with friends _____
A sensuous sex life _____
A large library of books _____
Peace in the world _____
To be treated fairly _____
Confidence in yourself _____
Influence and power in your community _____
A high spiritual experience _____
A satisfying religious faith _____
Dependable transportation _____
Someone who needs you _____
Someone to take care of you _____
Orderliness in your affairs _____
A close-knit family _____
Wealth _____
Other _____

3. What is important to you in your actual work conditions? (Rate on a scale of one to ten.)

To work alone _____
Regular hours and guaranteed pay _____
A totally unstructured work day _____
Self-employment _____
Good supervision _____
Having a variety of tasks _____
Work in a small organization _____
Outdoor work _____
Opportunity for overtime _____
Little responsibility and risks _____
Short commute _____

4. Choose three things from the choices below that give you the most satisfaction in your work.

To be excited by what you're doing _____
To help others solve problems _____
To contribute to society with worthwhile work _____
To be recognized as an authority _____
To motivate yourself _____
To figure things out _____
To work within a structured situation _____
To think through new solutions _____
To have choice about time _____
To make a lot of money _____
To work in a team atmosphere _____
To work outdoors _____
To be respected for your work _____
Other _____

5. Out of the five principal personality values, which ones do you

mainly identify with?

Theoretical: These people have a principal interest in discovering truth without judgment. They mainly want to observe and reason.

Economic: These people value first what is useful and practical. They feel unapplied knowledge is a waste.

Aesthetic: These people take the most pleasure from the artistic episodes of life. They love form and harmony.

Social: The highest value for this personality is the love of people.

Political: These people tend to desire influence, fame, and power first and foremost.

6. Name your five top values, based on your answers.

Over the next few months, observe if your desires change. Do these new desires reflect a change in values? Values change very slowly. Even though at the rational level we decide to be different, our automatic responses, based on old values, often lag behind. As your goals and values become more congruent, you become more powerful, for then you are not in conflict with yourself.

WHAT DO I WANT? TECHNIQUES

The closer we are to being the directors of our lives, the more in touch we feel with our dreams and desires. We need now to let go and daydream a little. It's very useful to establish a daily program of taking a few minutes to think, write, read, and meditate on goals. Some of these suggestions may help structure that time, which should be approached in an easy, relaxed manner:

1. List all the major areas of you life. What do you want in the areas of love, home, work, play, health, finance, career, independence,

travel, recreation, self-confidence building, personal growth, relationships, closeness with God?

2. Ask yourself questions and keep a diary of your answers:

    a. List what you don't want.

    b. List what you "should want" according to the significant people in your life.

    c. What hasn't lived yet in your life?

    d. What have you always wanted to do someday?

    e. What would you do if you could do anything you wanted for a year?

    f. How much money would you like to be making in a year? In five years?

3. Daydream a little. Long-hidden wants sometimes reveal themselves in intuitive flashes. They rarely show you the whole plan, or show the whole yellow brick road. Ideas come and go quickly in the form of images. Write them down. The dullest ink lasts longer than the sharpest memory.

4. Turn envious thoughts to positive use. When you feel envy at someone's good fortune, know that this may be a signal for some want you have. Release the envy and keep the desire.

5. Create an image of the ideal for yourself. Remember, it's good to desire; wanting is a prerequisite for receiving. How would you ideally have your life? Put on some soft music, lie back, and imagine an entire ideal day:

    Where would you be living? With whom?

    Where would you be working? Under what circumstances?

    How would you be playing? Loving? Being?

    Now open your eyes. How is your ideal different from your reality today? Keep a journal of your thoughts.

6. Learn to pick a bouquet of roses from the thorn bushes in your life. Inside every dissatisfaction is a want. When you're experiencing any negative emotion, keep asking yourself, "What do I want?" Avoid the inclination to just remain upset. Remind yourself that

the world is yours for the asking — but you must know exactly what you want.

What you have been doing so far is creating prosperity goals in general terms. Before they become specific, they need to survive a series of other questions. Observe your intentions and reactions as you ask yourself:

Have I dared to think big enough?
Is my goal based on pure fantasy?
Is it achievable, believable, and measurable?
Is the goal life-producing?
Does it hurt any others?
Does this goal really belong to me?
Is it legal?
Is it good for all concerned?
Do I have the consciousness of having this goal?
Can I see myself already having it?
Have I investigated what I will need to do to have this goal (such
     as education, experience)?
Am I willing to undertake the undesirable aspects of the job?
Can I handle the rewards of getting this goal?
Am I willing to take on the responsibility of this goal?

At first, tell no one about your desires. Later, you may want feedback about how others see your project, but when you are initially building your confidence and accepting your own decisions as valuable, give your ideas time to germinate. Getting a negative response from others too soon might cause you to release it prematurely. You do not want to put yourself in a position of explaining or justifying your desires and ideas while they are still fresh and new to you. Let them develop strength of their own before you share them.

GOALS THAT CREATE

So far, we've been thinking about general goals, but definite results require definite ideas. For plans to succeed, we need to make our general goals concrete.

In defining a goal, we choose to focus energy in concentrated form on a certain event or thing. With this focus comes the strength and power to create what we want. We are now ready to go beyond the usual, "I want to be happy," or "I want someone to love me," and specify what would make us content, or what characteristics we'd like to find in a partner. We need to know as precisely what we desire as possible.

Wishing is only a start. As a vaguely conceived goal it will be vaguely expressed. The statement, "Wouldn't it be nice if . . ." shows little energy behind it. Wishes need to be made into declaratives in clear, concise words.

"Should" goals are in the same category. Unless we're acting on our shoulds, they are only for show anyway. By repeating the thought, "I should write my mother every week," we can prove our good intentions, and still continue not to write Mother. Shoulds have little generative energy to change behavior. First, you must become clear on what kind of communication you want with your mother and how often you want it. Your goal then comes from what you really want.

INTENSE DESIRES ARE CREATIVE DESIRES

Powerful, impelling goals have the full force of the self emerging from bondage. Expressing these desires brings a distinct bodily reaction — a "feeling response" that we can't miss. We've all had that experience of being extremely clear about some strong desire, and knowing it was ours long before it was actually manifested.

At such times, the world seems to be our oyster. We can literally see, smell, taste, touch success. We're not at all surprised when we succeed — it just seems natural.

A friend recently told me she "knew" a certain job was hers when she received the call for an interview. She felt it was just a matter of showing up. She was right; she got the job that day.

Another young couple in Chicago made newspaper headlines when they won a large sum of money in a lottery. There had been no doubt at all about the rightness of this goal for them. They were in desperate financial straits and had decided they had to win that lottery. They spent several hours each day meditating, intensely visualizing winning — what it would feel like when the phone rang, when the check arrived, depositing it and spending it. They reported later that it was almost anticlimactic to actually win the lottery because they had deeply experienced even the joy of winning.

We have many levels of desires. By sorting through and finding out which ones are truly coming from our deepest well, we will tap into the energy we need to help create it physically. We don't have to force our minds to concentrate on something we deeply want and feel we deserve — it just happens naturally.

Take a moment and re-create a time when you experienced that power of knowing deeply what you wanted, and got it. Take a deep breath, relax, and go back in memory to a time when you sensed something you really wanted was going to happen, although to all outward appearances there was no way to know it. Feel the knowing in your body. Pay attention to the thoughts you were having. Remember the details of where you were, and what happened. Remember how you looked and felt. This "feeling response" when you know your goal is on target is your success signal.

When you have that feeling response of winning, you know you have chosen your goal well. You are in alignment with your feelings, values, desires, and you have eliminated all negative opposition in your own thoughts. And a paradox now comes into play.

THE MAGIC PARADOX

Our prosperity task is to be *specific* about our goals and plans to achieve our goals. In other words, we're programming our subconscious through the use of our conscious mind. At the same time that we are working with specifics, however, we must also stay aware that our subconscious does not deal with specifics. The subconscious responds to the essence of that which we desire.

So, while the subconscious must be programmed with exact detail, our higher intelligence, manifesting through our subconscious, is drawing from a whole warehouse of universal consciousness and is not limited by our requests. The results are not always exactly the way we think we want them. The answers to our problems may come about in ways we never dreamed possible. We all know miracle stories of chance meetings with a stranger who held the perfect answer for a pressing problem or need. Once we hand a problem over to Infinite Intelligence, we must stay alert to the possibilities constantly opening up around us from our source — Infinite Intelligence — in the form of creative ideas and situations.

There are few shortcuts to prosperity consciousness. It is only after we have defined what we want in definite terms that we become aware of all the possible ways of receiving what we desire. In that sense, prosperity consciousness can be seen as a process of *waking up*. We are responding to a higher self, that part of us that knows we deserve what we want. This helps to explain the paradox that while we must be specific, and desire our goal intensely, we must also let go of the idea of having to have the exact thing in the exact way we think it should happen. We must stay open to our original idea, or something better.

Knowing what you want in life is a reward itself. Spend as much time alone with your thoughts as possible, for this is internal work. No one can help you with your true desires. This is a wonderful game of consciousness and, played well, will result in attracting your life of abundance.

12

PLANNING YOUR SUCCESS

Becoming prosperous is first of all being truthful to ourselves.

PROSPERITY LAW NO. 3:
THE LAW OF PLANNING

Without planning there is no consistent prosperity.

*T*he three most important secrets of success are planning, planning, and planning!

By planning you are giving detailed attention to your intention. Once you have established your overall goals, you will want to make specific plans for achieving your goals in all the important areas of your life: home, work, finances, recreation, health, and relationships. Start by writing one goal that you want to achieve in five years for each major area of your life. This helps you to look at the whole picture and see how the separate goals fit together. The object is to maintain balance in your life, and not get lopsided or carried away in any one interest to the exclusion of the rest.

FINANCIAL PLANNING

One major area women are awakening to is the need to plan for financial independence. You will first need to understand your financial situation today and determine how much money you will need to fulfill your goals. Less than five percent of U.S. citizens sixty-five years of age are financially independent; seventy-five percent are dependent upon others (family, friends, welfare); the rest still need to work. The National Council on Aging estimates that the total liquid assets per capita of all people sixty-five years of age (mostly women) are approximately $3,500.

A woman earning $15,000 a year for thirty years earns a total of almost half a million dollars. Unless she manages it well, however, she will end up with about as much as she started. We need to learn to live on ninety percent of whatever we bring home. Most of us do the opposite. As our income increases, so do our expenditures — or worse — we become heavily in debt for items of immediate consumption. Financial advisors tell us that the only good reason for borrowing money is to make money. If we borrow for consumer items the debt lasts much longer than the items — often they've broken down, worn out, or we've gotten rid of them long before they're paid off. Being in debt for items we have already consumed can be debilitating psychologically, and we can end up feeling trapped financially.

Becoming prosperous is first of all being truthful to ourselves. It means taking responsibility for our financial state. To do this, you will need to list in a budget book all outstanding debts, monthly expenditures, and income. Next, list all assets and liabilities that are liquid and not liquid to give you a net worth picture. Establish a payment plan on your debts that assures you a good credit rating. If you cannot pay fully, speak to your creditors and arrange a pay-back schedule you can afford. It may mean temporarily lowering your standard of living, and not buying those items you dearly want right now — but very quickly a peace of mind and an excitement about future potential develops. This feeling cannot be bought.

What do you do with the ten percent? That's the second golden rule of money: Pay yourself first. Skim ten percent right off the top of your income to pay yourself. You deserve it. That is yours to keep. It is your investment money; envision it as your past labor that continues to work for you. You will want to invest that money safely and to continue to reinvest the interest it earns. Never plan on spending your original investment money. Have a separate account for savings to purchase your bigger items. This investment money is used only to accumulate interest and to help build your financial independence.

The truth is that no one has ever gotten wealthy from a salary. There are not enough hours in the day, or enough strength in the body to earn great wealth. Money invested safely with compound interest, however, never stops working.

A prospering woman must develop a consciousness of investing. We all know we need to earn money; we now need to learn what to do with it after we've earned it. It's not that hard. There are only a few areas we can invest in: savings, real estate, stocks and bonds, precious metals, stones, and collectibles. You need to learn the risks and opportunities involved in each area. There are many free investment seminars to attend; some investment counselors will also provide the first hour free to discuss individual financial situations. Professional help is important, but all final decisions must be yours, for you are responsible for them.

The way we invest depends upon many things: how much money we need to live the way we desire; how long we want to work; our level of anxiety; and how much we're willing to risk to get what we want. Becoming money conscious is time consuming, but so is work.

YOUR PLAN

For overall life plans, ask yourself, "How do I want to be living five years from now? What needs to happen in four years to reach that five-year plan? In three years? Two years?" Outline your goals in detail for next year. What can you do by next month? Next week? This week? Today?

Be truthful and realistic in your planning. Establish a daily pattern of starting each day by reviewing your weekly goals and deciding one thing you can do every day toward achieving each goal. Remember that the whole idea of planning is to keep your mind focused in a positive way on where you are heading. It doesn't matter how big your steps are — what matters is that you take them.

13

RELEASING TO PROSPER

"If you want greater prosperity in your life,
start forming a vacuum to receive it!"
— Catherine Ponder

PROSPERITY LAW NO. 4:
THE LAW OF RELEASING

We must get rid of what we don't want
to make room for what we do.

*E*very successful person knows and practices the law of release in some form or other. He or she knows that to be prosperous, the outgrown, worn out, used up, bypassed, outlasted must be discarded. When you have decided which ideas, relationships, beliefs, and situations no longer work for you, it is time to release them. Nothing stays new, shiny, or useful very long among unwanted dusty, old, cluttered, stored items.

The first area of release is with yourself. One way to stay open to the flow of life energy is to see yourself as a temple composed of body, mind, and spirit. Your body is your base, holding the structure

129

together. Your mind is your communicator with your spirit, and your spirit is your connection with infinite energy. Keeping this temple open to receiving requires release in all three areas — body, mind, and spirit.

BODY CLEANSING

Health and balance in the body is necessary for any true prosperity. We have our own inner doctor always available for consultation. You can do a quick checkup by periodically asking yourself these questions:

1. Are you at the weight that makes you feel best?
2. Are you eating the fresh fruits, vegetables, and whole grains you need, or are you primarily eating too many "dead" processed foods?
3. Are you exercising daily: stretching for muscle tone and actively exercising for increased heartbeat and circulation? We are moving creatures — it is almost impossible to remain in a depressed state while actively moving in a body made firm, flexible, and relaxed by adequate exercise.
4. Can you relax? A tense muscle is a weak muscle. Muscles become strong by tensing and releasing. We are usually very good at tensing; all too often we don't know how to release in healthy ways. Alcohol and drugs will help to release tension temporarily, but the price is outrageous.

Give yourself permission to relax. Relaxing is not a sign of laziness; it is a sign of intelligence. When we tense and release, we are in step with the pulse of the universe. By fully letting go of tension in the muscles, we are making room for fresh new blood to bring nutrients to the entire system, thereby increasing our energy level and promoting greater productivity.

MIND CLEANSING

The most important release for the mind is letting go of negative thoughts. We all have these thoughts visiting us — but we are not stuck with them. Putting out the Not Welcome sign doesn't work too well; they keep coming.

We are only stuck with negative thoughts when we feed them by giving them our attention. Positive thinking alone doesn't work because we become emotionally attached to our negative thoughts. How do we "let go" of negative attitudes (thoughts) when we don't feel positive?

It helps to remember that thoughts come before feelings. If you can stay aware enough, you can catch the thought that leads to feeling low. Check it out the next time you feel slightly down: What were you saying to yourself just before your spirit started its downward slide?

Becoming aware of, and dwelling upon, negative thoughts are two different things. The philosopher William James had this to say on handling negative feelings:

To wrestle with a bad feeling only pins our attention on it, and keeps it still fastened in the mind. Whereas, if we act as if from some better feelings, the old bad feeling soon folds its tent like an Arab, and silently steals away.

SPIRIT CLEANSING

When we cleanse the spirit, we renew our sense of universal harmony. It is an activity both refreshing and rewarding. Start each morning by giving yourself a gift of ten to fifteen minutes to be by yourself. The busier you are, the more important it is that you take this time.

Close your eyes and be aware of the newness of each day, and of who you are in the universe. Give thanks for your oneness with all there is. This process opens you to your prosperity consciousness, where you recognize that what you want wants you. By taking this consciousness into your daily activities, you make life an ongoing cleansing and healing meditation.

FINISHING CYCLES

Once we start this cleansing motion of releasing body, mind, and spirit, we will find it fun and easy because it is a circular action. The more we experience peace and order within, the more we demand it in our environment.

As we start today working toward having life more centered, focused, and peaceful, we will want to clean up the house, our car, our clothes, the office. We'll want to clear out all that is no longer useful, including old clothes, dishes, furniture, whatever; straighten up drawers; clean out our closets, the garage, the attic, the storeroom; balance the checkbook; finish the incomplete things in our lives. This may require taking care of those small tasks that have been a constant irritant, running those errands, making those calls we've been putting off. It may mean deciding to repair or get rid of broken items. Unfinished cycles prevent us from experiencing peace, order, and harmony in our physical and mental world.

This is also garbage can time for old ideas, beliefs, and relationships that are not working. Assumptions that are not bringing joy, such as "I *have* to cook every night" may be ready for the can. Develop the sense that you do what you do by *choice* — for that is the truth. I don't have to exercise; I choose to feel fit.

Worn out worries and doubts go, too. They only serve to hold you back, and get rancid when they've been around too long. Put all the old problems that wouldn't be solved into that same garbage can — and release them, with love, letting go without further judgment or attachment.

Letting go of relationships that hold toxic energy for you is important, too. If good energy is gone in a relationship and neither of you is contributing to the other's growth, decide to tell the truth about why you are hanging on. Acting out of fear or lethargy is the opposite of moving creatively toward your joy.

RELEASING RESENTMENT

Another aspect of cleansing is learning to forgive yourself and others. One of the most important keys on your prosperity key chain is the following prosperity key.

PROSPERITY KEY NO. 8
Forgive all who have offended you — not for them, but for yourself.

We do not need to wait until others deserve our forgiveness, because we're not doing it for them. By holding resentments against others, we hurt ourselves more than anyone else. Clinging to our resentments is like taking poison every day. Why do we continue it?

Here's a little secret that may help you to give up resentments. Think about this: If a tiger were chasing you across the field, hell-bent on eating you, would you be focusing on how much you were resenting having to run to safety? Probably not! Yet you would have every reason to. You are not at fault; something out there is doing it to you; you feel helpless; you have no choice. Why don't you resent it?

We only resent situations in which we know, deep down, we could have reacted differently. We could have done something other than what we did. In other words, it is really ourselves and our actions (or lack of action) that we resent. We don't resent the tiger, because tigers will be tigers. We are doing all we can do, which is to get out of the tiger's path.

To forgive and let go of resentments, therefore, we need to ask ourselves what our input into any given situation was — what could we have done differently than what we did do? Realizing that we do have input in almost every situation puts us back into our sense of personal power — and releases that terrible feeling of being victimized.

We can also learn to bless others — even our "enemies." Coming from the attitude that there is a lesson in every problem, we can see that our opponent has just helped us to learn faster. It is therefore to our advantage to forgive and even thank this person for this opportunity. After all, we're not victimized saints — we're always doing the best for No. 1 (according to our insight at the time) every step of the way — and so is the other guy (or gal).

The more we can forgive and bless with goodwill, the faster we are opening the channels to our prosperity. But it can't be phony. You have to really forgive — to recognize that the essence of the other person is the same as yours.

Forgiving ourselves and others is our single biggest step toward prosperity consciousness, exceeded only by the need to let go of negative thought.

HOW DO YOU START?

Ask your Inner Guidance, "Who do I need to forgive?" Often we're not aware of being unforgiving. Listen to yourself talk. Every time you hear resentment in your voice, know you've found someone or something else to put on your forgiveness list.

An excellent way to truly forgive is to:

1. Imagine that you are speaking to the person who has offended you.
2. Ask her or him to forgive you for holding negative feelings about him or her.
3. Visualize that person surrounded in a white light that protects his or her well-being.

If you find you cannot find it in your heart to forgive, know that your inner self has already forgiven and you can tap into the strength of that forgiving spirit. A good statement to make while visualizing this is "My inner self forgives you."

The warm feeling you receive in your own heart as your ability to love increases is reward in itself. But you will find that as you increase your loving responses to the world, that you will also be miraculously effecting changes in the attitude of others toward you!

GIVING WITH LOVE

Another phase of the cleansing process is learning to give generously of your resources. We must always give before we receive. This is an old adage every successful businessperson knows and puts into action. Never pass up a chance to give.

Giving is not restricted to just money. There is always something we can give, even if we are on the tightest of budgets. It may seem impossible to give when our entire attention is on the need to receive, but it is expressly at those times when we feel needy that we will benefit the most from giving.

Feeling scarcity can be very depressing, and when our energy begins to spiral down into depression our prosperity prospects spiral downward also. Our first task is to increase that energy level. One way to do this is to give. It lifts our spirits to give.

Giving is simpler than we think. We all have a variety of skills and talents that can contribute to others' well-being. Even a smile is worth a million to the right person at the right moment. Being kind, helpful, and considerate toward others with what we have reminds us of our oneness with all of life.

The outside world is only a reflection of our inside world. The only one we're ever dealing with is ourselves. Giving convinces our subconscious that we already have more than we need. We are prosperous, and expect to continue to be so.

The bottom line then, is that when we give, we benefit. It is time to give up the martyr role of giving as a sacrifice. Everything we do in life is for ourselves first. If another person benefits from our good deeds — that's icing on the cake — nice, but of less importance. That's not being selfish; it's telling the truth.

By acknowledging how much we receive by doing our "good deeds," we free up the receiver of our gifts from any guilt. Again, we need to thank others for the opportunity to give, because it makes us feel so good!

PROSPERITY KEY NO. 9
Spend your money with the consciousness of giving with love.

It is my contention that human beings are created with the potential for immense understanding and love, but because most of us are unaware of this, we must learn about it through every action we take. Nowhere do we learn faster than through our money trip.

Money problems are a mirror reflection of consciousness problems, because when we are dealing with money we get to see ourselves in context. How you deal with money is a reflection of how you see yourself in the world.

When we spend consciously, it is love in action. When we spend unconsciously we are headed for first-class trouble. So much spending is associated with loss, and done begrudgingly. We want to reach the place where we can give with the same attitude we wish to receive from others — with love and goodwill.

Because money is what the human race values above all else, money has power — lots of power — and it can hurt when that power boomerangs. Ask anyone who has gone into debt and has not been able to stop spiraling down. Ask anyone who has embezzled "just a little," to get by on. Ask anyone who's been living on the edge from paycheck to paycheck so long she feels her life is like a piece of Swiss cheese and the holes are getting bigger.

Is there an attitude, an approach to money, that allows us to see a different picture of ourselves? When we're going to buy something, how many times do we stop to ask ourselves:

What do I really want?
What will it do for me?
Is this something I need to buy?
Is there a better way?
How much will it cost in life force energy?
Am I willing to pay the price?
What will I have to do to earn this money?

Usually we either close our eyes and pay the money before we think twice, or if we don't have the money or the credit, quickly discount our dreams and fall into a depressive feeling because we can't have (whatever). From this point of view it is easy to see how we give away our power and instead feel the "if only" blues — that money is the answer to all our dreams.

I believe it is necessary to master the game of money — to know how to make money happen in our life — both how to earn it and spend it wisely, before we can give it up.

To live prosperously is to live with integrity: mentally, physically, emotionally, spiritually, and financially. Prosperity does not mean to live beyond our means — to borrow, beg, or steal. It does not mean to go into debt or to spend more than we have.

To live prosperously means to be *honest* about our money — spend less than we earn; to pay ourselves first (savings); to pay our bills on time (or keep in regular contact with creditors until we are able to pay); and to buy only what we need to be happy and fulfilled.

Let go of negative thoughts when you are spending money. Acknowledge to yourself the spiritual nature of money, and know that as you give, so you receive. Bless the money as a symbol of the unlimited supply of the universe. Tell yourself that *twice* that amount is now on its way to you.

By focusing your thoughts on prosperity instead of loss, you are convincing your subconscious that you are really serious about being prosperous. As a prosperous woman your supply will always be replenished. When you assume the attitude and behavior of a prosperous woman, you become one, through the action of the subconscious.

Did you ever hear of the Peace Pilgrim? She was a wonderful older woman who walked from town to town taking nothing with her but her inner glow of love. She spoke all over the country about the beauty and freedom of owning less. I got to hear her twice when she came through the little town in Oregon where I lived. Her message was very inspirational and I never forgot it. Possessions, she said, can be a heavy burden.

The law of releasing is often overlooked, yet it is the basis of being ready for all the more appropriate good that is on its way to us. What we already have is often obscured by living in clutter. If we do not continually put our house in order, there is no space for anything new. When we feel our space clogged, *more* satisfies *less*.

Releasing, on the other hand, actually creates a vacuum — a space to breathe. We have a way to think clearly, see what is important, and plan for the next step. No vacuum remains empty long. This vacuum is no exception. It literally pulls our desired results to us.

Simply put, prosperity requires a balance of giving and receiving, and both must be done from a place of love. Spending and giving must be done with prosperity consciousness, an awareness of what is being spent or released as well as what is being taken in. As you picture yourself in the center of a joyous network of giving and receiving with love and wisdom, you'll soon see yourself in the circular world of prospering energy.

PROSPERITY PROFILE NO. 8

Interview with Reverend Marcia Sutton, Ph.D., a previous minister of the Golden Gate Church of Religious Science in the San Francisco Bay Area.

Q: Where do spirituality and prosperity meet?

A: There are really two ideas that come to mind — abundance and prosperity. They are both qualities of God, present all around us. We are here to individualize these expressions of God. We are the point, the area, where prosperity and spirit meet.

Abundance is an enduring quality of God. We can live a prosperous life, and have what we need, when we need it. We can have a sense that we already have enough. We can have a spiritual relationship with money, and with God. It all comes down to relationships. You can have a little money and a life of freedom and plenty of abundance. You can have plenty of money and experience very little freedom.

Q: How do you experience that abundance?

A: I can feel prosperous in many ways; in relationships, in my experience of time, and in my attitude of freedom. I can feel I am enough, and feel I have enough. When I'm feeling limitation and lack, I like to look to the higher life expression of God. I go out at night and look at the stars, and by looking at the stars I get a direct expression of God's abundance. If it's during the day I'll sit and look at a tree; a tree never needs more leaves. If they fall off, they come back in another season. The other place I go is by the water. I become conscious of the grains of sand — I can see sand and beach for miles. The grains of sand, the leaves, the stars, all remind me of that quality of God which is abundance.

We are that place where God becomes individualized. When we want to have a better relationship with God, something in us then opens up, and there is a circulation of that expression which opens up better ideas, greater gifts, greater good, and more money, but it's not limited to money. We can focus on being the place of expression for any quality that we associate with God, such as abundance, freedom, peace, love, joy, or power. Being in a right relationship to the quality of God that is abundance is what I think this book is about.

Q: How do we make a switch from our ongoing relationship with our problems of money or lack, to changing our attention and having a relationship with an abundant God?

A: So often we spend a lot more time thinking about our problems than we do thinking about God. You might say we have a closer relationship with our problems than we do with God. Let me give you an example.

In 1987 I literally lost everything financially. I had given up my career, my house, my husband, and I was devastated. I had overspent and become disorganized, and I was brought to my knees. It was then I opened the door to my spirituality. I sought to have a relationship with the Higher Life, which I now call God. That old life, built out of ignorance, had to come crumbling down. I started attending a Religious Science church and I began reading, and I came across this idea of a universal presence of a good God, which was new to me. I saw there was more to life, and I began feeling it.

This difficult transition happens with a lot of people who are having money problems. Not everyone has a financial crisis; it can be a health problem, or a relationship failure, or many other kinds of challenges that bring us to our knees. Old things need to be released — old ideas don't work and so they need to get broken up. From this we are invited to start looking for new answers.

Q: What happened after your transition?

A: I had two important experiences at that time of transition. One, I realized that if I had to walk from San Diego to Los Angeles to attend ministerial school, with just the clothes on my back, and leave everything behind, I would do it. Willingness created a shift in me and I was given an opportunity to continue. Second — I began the spiritual practice of tithing, the act of giving. At that time I only earned six hundred dollars a month, and 10 percent was a lot to give away. I had little, and yet I felt if I never took this step I would never know, never experience for myself what would happen, and I wanted to teach about it. I had to try it and know for myself.

From that moment my life got better in many ways. It took time, but that greater relationship with God opened up my own givingness. I also became open to receive. Gradually over time, healing took place in my consciousness, and then outwardly, pictured in my life.

When we're confronted with a major challenge, we take what we know intellectually and go from "talking" to "walking." We bring our thoughts into our hearts. Out of those challenges, we discover the presence of God. We ask, "Will God guide me?" And somewhere in the process, we discover a place within ourselves that touches God. So, it becomes our responsibility to nurture this place, and thus nurture our relationship with God. We can set aside time to be in this relationship, time to talk or to be quiet and allow the guidance to be revealed. The way we listen to God is through meditation, and the way we talk to God is through prayer. Then, there comes a moment when you feel the quality of God alive in you; you feel it in your body; you feel balanced.

Q: So prosperity is finding the right relationship with God?

A: Yes, prosperity is coming home to a deeper truth. It's nothing more than having an experience of being enough, so that we know there is enough for us. It always comes back to our own attitude — if our attention is being pulled to, "there's not enough," then our experience will produce circumstances that show us there "isn't enough."

On the other hand, the spiritual journey invites us to realize that in God there is enough. So, the key is in our being in a right relationship with God. To change our thinking in this way is a courageous act. Yet, this silent act that takes place within us always brings us closer to God, and from here, everything changes.

14

YOU PAY FOR WHAT YOU GET

"Material good has its tax, and if it came without desert or sweat,
has no root in me, the next wind will blow it away.
"Has a man gained who has received a hundred favors and rendered
none? Always pay. If you are wise you will dread a prosperity which
only loads you with more. He is great who confers the most benefits."

— Ralph Waldo Emerson

PROSPERITY LAW NO. 5:
THE LAW OF COMPENSATION

There is a price for everything and we always pay.

While it is true that we continually receive abundantly from the universe, it is also true that there is no such thing as a free lunch. What we often want to ignore is the tax that comes with the gifts. We pay for everything we receive in life, and that includes prosperity.

The gift and the price are more often called the law of cause and effect, out of which probably came the sage remark, "Be careful of what you want, you might get it." The reason for concern is legitimate. Whatever we receive has a multitude of effects. It is good to think through what those effects might be, and ask if the price is too high. For example, conditions around your job may be so unsatisfactory, you think you want out. Are you willing to pay the price of being out of work tomorrow to satisfy your desire to quit now?

We appreciate most what we have to pay for; and therefore the law of compensatory action really works to our advantage. Making payment for what we want jars us out of our waking sleep. When we realize the cost of our choices, we come alive for the moment to see what we have purchased. Identifying the price we will have to pay for each of our desires can actually help us promote our state of conscious alertness. We need to ask ourselves if we truly want our goals enough to pay the tax — for pay we will, in money, effort, time, and peace of mind. As we gradually accept that we do pay, we tend to choose our wants more wisely. The law of compensation applies to all — it is a universal law. Yet it doesn't always seem to. When we observe dehumanizing, brutal, corrupt, or otherwise lawless acts going unpunished, we often ask ourselves if such acts, or individuals, are exempt from the law. We begin to doubt that a law of retribution exists.

But what we don't very often see is the cancerous effect on the insides of those individuals who gain at the high cost to others. Human beings, by nature, are ethical beings. We pay where it counts most — in our guts — when we deviate from what we know to be right action. We never "get away with" anything, because we cannot leave ourselves. We may try, with alcohol, drugs, overeating, and other escapist activities, but we must always return to ourselves. We are our own persecutors. The hell that rages within is a far greater punishment than any penalty which a court of law can inflict. The anger that is expressed outwardly is merely a reflection of the anger that is felt within at oneself.

Because the rectification of "wrong action" is not always immediately obvious, many people have been sold on the idea that the "bad" are successful and the "good" are miserable, but justice will be served in the hereafter. Ralph Waldo Emerson disagrees. In his essay, "Contemplation," he sees that the world balances itself perfectly.

Things refuse to be mismanaged long. Though no checks to a new evil appear, the checks exist. . . . All infractions of love and equity in our social relations are speedily punished. They are punished by fear . . . any departure from simplicity . . . or good for me that is not good for him, my neighbor feels the wrong; he shrinks from me as far as I have shrunk from him. . . . He indicates great wrongs which must be revised.

Because of the dual constitution of the things, in labor as in life there can be no cheating. The thief steals from himself. The swindler swindles himself.

In pursuit of our own prosperity, then, we need to constantly stay aware of our intentions toward others. Remember that the universal laws work on cause and effect — impersonally. If our intentions are not good for all concerned, all parties feel the negative effects. It is as if there is a third silent partner to all our actions. We cannot cheat others unnoticed, for we are creatures of integrity and are always watching ourselves.

Fortunately, right action — action based on integrity — works on this same principle of cause and effect. The price of extending love, knowledge, beauty, and wisdom to others is that we receive more of the same for ourselves.

Sometimes, with time and distance, we are able to see the big picture and observe the law of compensation at work. The best way to observe this is to be aware of how this works in our own lives. We all know examples of individuals being recipients of an outpouring of love when they least expected it. A friend of mine, for example, broke her leg and was given a Mercedes convertible with automatic shift to drive for the duration of her convalescence by someone who appreciated her loving way of being.

Sometimes we want to receive without giving, or receive without earning. Material gain does not benefit us if we have a "grab all you can while the grabbing is good, no matter who gets hurt" philosophy. As prospering women we must be in balance with the rest of the world — receiving that which we desire and helping others to benefit at the same time. If we continue to think about what is possible, look for our lessons in both our positive and negative experiences, combine love with wisdom in our actions toward others, and intend good for all concerned, we can count on experiencing the best that life has to offer. The beauty of this law is in its positive effects; we become tomorrow tenfold what we are today.

15

ATTRACTING YOUR PROSPERITY

*Be the qualities you want in your life and
you'll attract more of the same to you.*

PROSPERITY LAW NO. 6:
THE LAW OF ATTRACTION

We attract what we are.

We don't need a crystal ball to know our future. We are attracting our future through our consciousness now. We are our consciousness, and the quality of thought we hold in our minds right now is attracting the quality of life we are heading toward. The law of attraction and the law of compensation are sister laws. In both cases, like attracts like — the quality of our energy attracts more of the same to us.

This attracting energy of our consciousness is expressed through our thoughts. Thought, with feeling, magnetizes. In order to be prosperous then, we must first feel prosperous. This reminds me of having to prime the old red pump when I lived on a farm as a child in Michigan. In order to get water on those cold winter mornings, we had to pour water down the pump first. On the days we hadn't saved any water to prime with, we melted snow to get it. So too, to increase our prosperity, we must start with what we've got.

And we have plenty. We all have enough to prime the pumps and start to feel prosperous. Our first appeal is to the conscious mind through and intellectual understanding of the importance of feeling positive about attracting our prosperity.

You do not have to be wealthy to feel prosperous. Prosperous feelings that radiate magnetic energy are not generated by the amount of money in your pocket — that feeling is beyond dollars and cents. Feeling prosperous comes from an inner glow — a sense that all is well in the universe, that everything is just the way it should be.

Imagine living your life with the sensation of being fully satisfied, and yet being open to the world. When we feel prosperous, we know we can handle any turn of events that might take place. We've got what it takes to live freely without worry or fear. We feel a loving energy when we both give and receive. With this valuable sense of prosperity, we are more versatile, able to switch roles, play different parts, and recognize life as the exciting adventure it is — a game to be enjoyed.

There is no one thing that needs to happen, no obstacle to get by to start feeling prosperous. It is possible to feel a touch of it this moment. All you need to do is close your eyes, relax, breathe deeply, and remember a time somewhere in your past when you were feeling on top of your problems. We have all had those moments of knowing the love and support of the universe all around us. Just by recalling those pleasant feelings, the chemistry of your body changes, and you can achieve that prosperous feeling temporarily.

While in this state of well-being, decide to mentally radiate those qualities, now, that you desire to achieve in your life. We do not need to wait until we have enough of anything in order to be happy. If it is true that we attract only what we are, then let's be all that we can be now.

Exactly how do we do that?

1. Think through, clearly, what your concept is of a truly prosperous woman. What qualities would she have?
2. List the characteristics you have now that you like in yourself, and want to expand upon.
3. List the kinds of people and situations that you wish to attract to yourself as a prospering woman. What qualities would you have in those around you?
4. Close your eyes and imagine yourself being that prospering woman as you have defined her. Feel yourself having the qualities you believe she would have.

Begin to sense what being prosperous is like for you. How would you act? What would you do? How would you handle problems? What would you have? How would others act toward you? Open your eyes and list those things you can do today to express a feeling of prosperity.

RADIATE WHAT YOU DESIRE

At first, when we choose to radiate the qualities that we desire to bring into our lives, we feel as if we are pretending. In truth, however, we feel like actresses only because we have not allowed those qualities to emerge before. *Remember that at the core of our being, we are already perfect.* We are only moving one step closer to our true nature by deciding to express our higher qualities now. The deeper feelings will follow as you start attracting others with those same qualities, and feel reinforced from the outside by your efforts.

Keep in mind that feeling prosperous is enjoying fully what you already have. Right now all of us have resources we are not using, resources that can be appreciated now, rather than gathering dust waiting for that rainy day, or when company comes. It's time to treat ourselves like company.

Now is the time to utilize your best: Give yourself the option of wearing your best — every day if you feel like it. Look like a million dollars on an ordinary Wednesday afternoon, use your best dishes for breakfast, put candles and flowers on the table with the toasted cheese sandwiches. Dress in a manner that makes you feel not only "appropriate," but super. Fashion ads tell us to buy their products for others' approval. Your own approval is worth a million times more. Many a salesperson knows the real benefit of looking good in a new suit is in how the customer feels inside. Looking our best keeps our spirits high. By coming from enthusiasm and a bright outlook, we attract success — whether it's in making a sale or meeting a new friend. We tend to see more of the opportunities around us, and by being "up" we attract positive people like us.

LIVING AS AN ART FORM

Living prosperously is living life as an art form. All it takes is the intention of getting the most out of life in a loving, giving way. I had a personal experience of this while living in a student housing village near a major West Coast college with two hundred other veteran families. Most of us were earning less than minimum wage and supporting our families of three or four people, and yet a prosperous feeling predominated among us.

Many of these student-parents were working toward a goal they wanted and believed in, and the majority were pulling together in mutual support. Living so closely, we learned how to give each other privacy without having to avoid each other. We learned to care and help without intruding.

A community preschool was established and run by the group to perpetuate their highest values in education. Individual homes were artistically decorated from garage sales and miscellaneous want ads.

Many students shared their skills in home crafts: cabinetry, auto repair, pottery making, basket weaving, and painting — all at a very low cost to each other. Yards were not fenced, and toys were often shared. Adults formed discussion groups on political issues and acted in concert for causes they felt were important.

Living there was a high experience, not from a prosperity feeling bought with dollars, but from the richness of living with a group of people whose mental attitude included the spirit of love and cooperation.

The secret to experiencing joy in life is loving what you have while you're working toward what you want.

PROSPERITY PROFILE NO. 9

Interview with Caro Ann Medeghini, artist and teacher of language arts, history, and art at a junior high school in Central California.

Q: Caro, you have a wonderful home, beautiful clothes, a great sense of humor, a nice family, and a good job — how did you achieve this wonderful prosperity?

A: Prosperity is a combination of contributing meaningful deeds to the world, and being internally happy with yourself, family, and friends. I like to use my talents in art and education; sharing my knowledge with others is very gratifying. I love to see my students excel artistically, and their enthusiasm is overwhelming.

Communication with my family and friends is very important. My openness with family and friends means a great deal to me. I generally say what I think — honesty and sincerity are the nucleus of friendship. My paintings are a means of expression (peaceful and tranquil), a sense of artistic accomplishment. Also, I try to listen well. I have an open ear. I care deeply about my friends and family, and they can trust me and my judgment. I have an open sense of listening. If you confide in me, our conversations will not go any further.

Q: When you were back in college, did you have a process for achieving your success?

A: My mom and dad were big influences in attaining my academic goals. My parents were hard workers who carried many financial burdens so that I could have a college education. At that time, I didn't understand their difficulties, until I experienced them myself. One crucial goal my parents instilled in me was that I was going to achieve more than they had achieved. They always stressed the positive, and good, strong values. They would remind me, "We know you'll succeed, but we will supervise your college years." As college was nearing the end and I wasn't sure what career I was going to follow, my mom suggested I follow in my great-grandmother's footsteps. She was an art teacher and artist. Needless to say, that decision has turned out to be very positive. I have experienced twenty-eight satisfying years in education. Good job Mom and Dad. I love you with all my heart.

Q: It seems that you had a lot of family support and positive messages about yourself as you grew up.

A: A lot of what I experienced during my formative years were the steps I needed to succeed. I experienced the usual array of ups and downs, but I always had nurturing and caring parents that were there for me.

I have a great deal of initiative inside me to do well. I give myself a lot of self-direction and I am focused, almost fanatic about the perfection of projects. If I have something in my mind, it's all I think about until it's done.

The most important thing in life is to remember to ask yourself, "What is it people will remember about me when I'm gone?" I do my best to live my life with that in mind.

16

PICTURE YOUR PROSPERITY

"Creative visualization is magic in the truest and highest meaning of the word. It involves understanding and aligning yourself with the natural principles that govern the workings of our universe, and learning to use these principles in the most conscious and creative way."

— Shakti Gawain

PROSPERITY LAW NO. 7:
THE LAW OF VISUALIZATION

We become what we imagine, positive or negative.

*R*eal wealth has always been made through acting upon creative ideas. Millions of new thoughts are born every minute; only a few take root and grow. How fully developed the idea becomes is dependent upon the imaginative energy spent on that seed idea. The first nurturing action in our creative process then has to be on our own mental work.

Up until now we have focused primarily on the use of words — verbal and nonverbal — to do this work. Yet every productive achievement must first be imagined in the mind. Creative visualization — mentally picturing with emotion — is another important tool we have for mind action. By combining words with feelings and images, we can be more effective in programming the subconscious to manifest conditions that we desire.

Many people feel they have little ability to imagine, or cannot visualize. Visualizing, however, is a natural but often unconscious process of the mind. We could not execute a normal day's activities without our ability to create mental images, for all thinking is done in some kind of conceptual imagery. For example, every single plan we make, whether it is to reorganize a business or make a shopping list, requires some sort of visualizing — perceiving in they eye of the mind that which is not yet visible to the physical eye.

Visualizing is also the natural process by which the mind communicates deeply buried feelings and beliefs. The importance of making this process conscious is that, without awareness, we usually choose to act according to the way we envision reality around us, not necessarily the way it actually is.

Much of our unconscious visualization comes in the form of fear images. For example, my daughter Kathy struggled with vivid "pictures" of horrible catastrophic events befalling her newborn baby. When she realized these images were expressions of fears that had the potential of creating actual negative experiences, she was able to focus on them in the light of rational expectations and let them go.

What we expect, believe, and picture, we usually get. Judging by all the negative expectations vividly portrayed in many of our conversations, it is amazing that we are able to create as much of the positive in our lives as we do. You can imagine what is possible once we have control of this power to create by deliberately visualizing ever more positive pictures.

The next step of concentrated mind action is choosing to do this very thing: to use this natural process of visualizing in a deliberate creative way to direct energy toward specific, positive purposes. When we consciously visualize, we are creating with picture-symbols — the language of the subconscious. We have greater access, therefore, to this powerhouse of manifesting energy. Picture-symbols, indirectly absorbed by the subconscious, represent not only our thoughts, but, used correctly, include information from all six senses — sight, sound, touch, smell, taste, and intuition.

VISUALIZING TECHNIQUES

The actual process of consciously creating imagery in the mind is much easier than you might guess. We all have an infinite capacity to produce bold, imaginative ideas and images in our own way. To prove to yourself that you can image at will, start with the easy stuff first. Relax a moment and close your eyes. Take a deep breath, see your favorite room at home. Walk all around it, touching objects, looking at the various colors in the room. Move a piece of furniture. Feel it under your hands.

What does the room smell like? Imagine yourself sitting in that room — how do you feel there? Try to get as total a picture as possible.

Next, let that scene go and imagine that you are holding a lemon in your right hand — a bright yellow, shiny lemon, about the size of your fist. Feel the rough texture of its skin. Smell it. Observe how it is shaped, with one end smaller than the other.

Now imagine cutting it in half. See a drop of juice pour out as you cut. Smell the pungent odor of the lemon. Take a bite out of one piece. Feel your mouth pucker. Spit the seeds out, and let yourself really taste the sour juice sliding down your throat. Now let that image go.

Imagine another scene — a happy time, a picnic, a time of a first love, a trip to the ocean — something you can easily recall visually with pleasure. Remember the details of that scene. Once again, look around you — what can you visually remember of that moment? Some people get more vivid "pictures" than others. You may get only a feeling sensation at first, or even just gray or black scenes. Relax into whatever is happening; there is no right or wrong way. Letting go of fear of worry that you can't visualize will often be enough to allow this natural phenomenon to occur.

Some people visualize best with their eyes open. Let your eyes go soft and gaze off into the distance, looking at nothing in particular, allowing your memory to recall the pleasant scenes mentioned earlier. What feels good and works is right for you. Everyone visualizes differently.

Just having the intention and putting your attention on visualizing a scene is enough to focus the power of the mind. Many people will immediately get some kind of picture sensations while recalling familiar scenes, even if they are very fuzzy at first. As you practice effective visualization, your ability to reproduce these scenes will increase proportionately.

To develop the ability to visualize, allow your eyes to outline objects several times during the day. Close your eyes, and see how much of the image you can retain. Repeat this often. Also, become more visually aware. Pay attention to color, design, shape, and the play of light and dark. Allow yourself to really look at details in plants, animals, nature, and people. Also try your hand at sketching to develop this inner seeing.

Discipline is required to train our imaginations to focus on details of our desires until they are clearly visible to the mind's eye. It is as important as developing the discipline we needed to observe the mind for negative thoughts.

This discipline is easy, rewarding, and fun, especially contrasted with the rigid rules for success most of us were brought up with in our culture. We were led to believe that the only way we could get what we wanted in life was to strive with a set jaw, and grind away at some detestable hard work. The grinding approach to success goes along with the collective negative thinking in our society that we will only appreciate good after we have suffered, that being rejected strengthens character, and that we need to constantly whip up our willpower to achieve more and more.

As always, there is a drop of truth in everything. Sometimes we do appreciate good after suffering, we do get stronger with rejection, and we do achieve more by beating on ourselves.

It does not follow, however, that willful striving is the way it has to be. Constant struggle is unnatural, ineffective, and inefficient.

THE ROLE OF WILLPOWER

When we attempt to force change, rather than allow change with imaginative mind action, we are trying to use willpower in a way it is not meant to be used. Emile Coue, an early pioneer in hypnosis for self-improvement, confirmed that imagination will always win out over will in any conflict. It is not the true nature of the will to fight. The will, rightly used, clarifies our purpose and directs our actions to carry out the desires of the conscious mind. Using willpower to force our behavior or that of others to conform to the ideas of the ego is based on fear, insecurity, and doubt. This is why resolutions using pure willpower don't work. When we try forcing our will from fear of doubt, we are bringing about the very thing we are trying to avoid.

Remember that *any* strong emotion, repeated often enough, programs the subconscious to create what we're thinking about. That includes strong negative feelings. Visual images caused by doubt, frustration, anger, worry — all negative emotions — hold back our good fortune and promote circumstances causing more frustration, anger, and worry.

Our only choice then is constant, careful, loving vigilance over the kind of program we set up in the subconscious with our current thoughts and mental images. By focusing on our desires, and on the pleasure our new patterns of life bring us, we are not fighting ourselves with our negatives. Our whole body is freed to move naturally in the direction we desire, attracting similar positive energy as we go along.

DIETING WITH IDEAL IMAGES

One example of the difference between allowing directed change and forcing change is in our approach to dieting. Diet by denial does not usually work on a long-term basis. What we resist persists. When we lose weight solely by not eating what we desire to eat, our minds focus constantly on the foods we're not eating. We call forth the rebellious child within by restricting our "goodies." We are not free for a moment; we're only tightening the bonds holding us to the prohibited foods.

True, these bonds are stretched as the foods are held out of our reach, but as soon as the final pound of weight is lost, and attention to the diet is relaxed, is it any wonder that we literally spring back to our original weight? We have not succeeded in moving on toward a new sense of being that includes being slim.

Visualizing allows us to experience how we want to be, act, dress, interact with others, feel, look, and generally how we want our new lifestyle to reflect a new inner feeling. When we practice being slim by visualizing it, the joy of seeing and feeling our slimness acts as a strong motivator keeping us on target.

PICTURING YOUR GOALS

By creating a visualization notebook, you can learn to focus your imagination on many positive goal images. Collect from various sources (old magazines, newspapers, greeting cards) symbols for what you want to create in your life. These can be in the form of pictures, sayings, statements, or symbols of any kind that catch your attention. Some pictures seem to literally jump off the page at us — these are the kinds of pictures you want. Tear them out without judgment — you don't have to defend your choices. Once you have a collection of these pictures, you will begin to see symbols or themes in them representing wants and needs in your life.

By now, having done the work suggested in this book, you will have identified the major areas in your life that are important to you (such as your home life, love life, and career), and established goals in each of those major areas. Create a page in your notebook for each important area of your life. Choose one goal to visualize for each of these areas. While you are learning, choose goals you can easily see yourself already achieving, goals for which you have a lot of enthusiasm, and ones that you absolutely expect to have.

Create your visualization notebook of brightly colored art paper. Choose colors that represent the qualities you want to bring into each area. For example, you might choose green for the financial page, and maybe rosy pink for health. Let the colors choose you — colors have a vibration of their own and actually have a subtle influence upon us. Label the goal of each page and paste an actual picture of you in the center.

Have fun and be as creative as you like with this notebook. On the financial page you may want to add some play money in large denominations. If any abstract images about goals come to you, draw them in your notebook. Sometimes drawing them with your non-dominant hand will help you overcome your own insecurity about your artistic ability. You will find gathering images and creating this notebook to be very enjoyable. Just in the act of doing it, your spirits will be uplifted.

The actual act of visualizing is most effective when done in a calm, easy manner, and with a positive frame of mind. For this reason, you will want to choose a time and place when you can be undisturbed. Allow your body to become relaxed, and clear your mind by letting go of all worry or anxiety, as well as all critical, judgmental thoughts. Try doing some simple stretches as a way to relax also.

Now, take deep abdominal breaths, letting your breath out in a slow, even, conscious stream, feeling more and more relaxed. Casually view the pictures you have cut out or drawn in your notebook. Lay them aside, and settle back. Pick a spot on the opposite wall on which to focus your full attention until your eyelids want to close. As you allow your eyelids to close, look up as if you were looking at the inside of your forehead. Pretend you are looking at the word RELAX printed across the inside of your forehead for a few moments, then release your eyes to return to their more normal position and feel a wave of relaxation flood your body. Taking a deep breath with each number, count backward from ten to one. Feel even more relaxed with each breath exhaled.

Now, recall the chosen goal for the day. Do not have more than one goal per day. When you find out how easy, pleasant, and effective programming the subconscious is, you will want to go inside with a shopping list, but resist the temptation. One goal per week works even better.

Allow images of achieving your given goal to form in your mind. Visualize each detail in a dreamlike state, using all your six senses. Breathe deeply and ask yourself how it would feel if you had already achieved your goal. Stay in this pleasant picture until you see yourself acting successfully. Visualize an entire day being your ideal self.

In other words, you are pretending you have already achieved your desires, and you are already feeling the warm glow of success in your body. Your subconscious only does what it is told, and with this process you are directing it, telling it you want more of this good feeling in your life. It will automatically get to work bringing it to you.

There are two basic kinds of meditative states of mind, and you use both when you visualize. One is the *participatory, active state* where you are outlining, and picturing to yourself exactly what you desire. You will also want to stay in a relaxed, quiet mood long enough for your higher self to speak back to you. Remain quiet a moment to hear any messages you need to hear. That is the *receptive state*. Both are necessary for manifestation, for producing what you desire.

Always end by giving thanks to the universe for all that you have received in the past which has made your life full and rich. Give thanks, also, for this new gift which is now on its way to you, remembering that it must be "beneficial for all concerned."

Finish by counting up from one to ten, bringing yourself back to your normal, energetic frame of mind. With each number, repeat, "Every day, in every way, I am healthier and healthier," or "I am more alive, awake, alert, enthusiastic." Open your eyes feeling relaxed, refreshed, ready and able to do whatever is necessary on your part to take your next step.

Keep an ongoing journal handy to record any insights and hunches that come up for you. Remember that creative ideas will come to you in flashes only — rarely is an entire plan revealed at once. We must be ready at all times to catch these creative thoughts that will open our way to wealth, health, and happiness.

There are many benefits of visualization. The mind is projected through time and space, unlimited by what seem to be obvious barriers. It is exhilarating, expansive, and practical to boot. Visualization allows us to move from the depressive state of limitation to the prosperous feeling of "I can!" It takes time for the mind to accept rich mental pictures, however. Be gentle with yourself. There is plenty of time.

The next chapter on affirmations explains how "statements of intention" contribute to the vortex of energy we are creating around us with our minds. It will be obvious how affirmations and visualizations go hand in hand, forming the perfect marriage, an unbeatable team. Provided you have done your homework — choosing your goals wisely and preparing to receive all the good that is ready to flow to you — you will now be able to create miracle after miracle in your life and in the lives of those around you.

17

DECLARE YOUR PROSPERITY

Speak to yourself as if what you desire is already true and it already is.

PROSPERITY LAW NO. 8:
THE LAW OF AFFIRMATION

*We become what we want to be by affirming and
acting on our belief that we already are there.*

*A*n affirmation is a positive thought held with conviction to produce a desired result. Effective affirmation is the act of stating
positively in written and oral form that which is yet to be. It is and act
of courage on the spiritual level, for it is a positive thought form in
the face of an unknown situation.

As you recall from earlier chapters, any thought held long enough
with intense feelings in the conscious mind will impress itself upon
the subconscious. Sufficiently impressed, the subconscious then has
no choice but to create for us what we desire.

Affirming by statement is a natural method of manifestation that we have been unconsciously using all along. Each of the 50,000 thoughts we have each day is actually an affirmation — positive or negative — and each is bringing about change in our lives accordingly. We don't have a choice of programming or not programming the subconscious. As long as we are thinking, we are doing it. We need to be aware of what we are programming! We want to assertively program positive thoughts so that we reap positive results.

Affirming is not the same as wishing. Wishing actually confirms doubt that this goal can happen. It is a passive expression of our desire. To affirm, on the other hand, is to make firm — to declare assertively that it is so. We are saying yes to our goal by affirming, rather than saying a wishful maybe.

The act of affirming that what we want is ours makes sense when we define our true nature as creative beings, and our true role in life as achieving an expanded awareness. We live in a supportive universe, overflowing with beautiful gifts. We are affirming only what is rightfully ours.

When you are just learning to affirm, it will be easier to maintain focus and develop skill in this technique if you choose goals that are well defined, truly desired, and that have enthusiastic energy behind them.

Vaguely conceived or vaguely worded goals leave us open to the cosmic humor. For example, at a recent prosperity conference, one woman related a story of her first attempt at affirmation. She had been a widow for some time. She decided to bring a man into her life, as she was lonely. Consequently she had been affirming "I want a man in the house." She did this for about a week. She got her desire all right, but not in the way she had intended. One day she walked into her house to find a burglar in the kitchen! She saw her error, and changed her affirmation to be more specific: "I want a man to love, who loves me and lives with me." She finally got what she really wanted and now has a loving relationship to come home to.

Affirmations and visualizations go hand in hand. You will want to choose and declare a goal through an affirmation that you can see yourself already having. You must hold in consciousness a $30,000-a-year job before you can effectively draw one from the universal warehouse. You must be able to see and feel yourself driving the car of your dreams, having the good relationship, or creating the corporate structure before you can attract them into your life on any permanent basis.

TECHNIQUES OF AFFIRMING

The process for stating an affirmation and following through is simple:

Write it:
1. State your desire specifically and intensely: "I now weigh 120 pounds, my ideal weight."
   Not: "I want to lose weight."
2. State it in a positive, active way: "I am now losing one pound a day."
   Not: "I am not fat."
3. State it as if it is already true: "Every day I look and feel great."
   Not: "I will be losing weight."
4. State it in a few words and to the point: "I now walk thirty minutes every day."
   Not: "I walk whenever I can, usually in the morning."

Use it:
1. Twice a day, repeat your affirmations out loud, five times each. Say them with enthusiasm, experiencing the joy of having received what you want.
2. Write your affirmations ten times each day with full attention and intention of receiving your goal.
3. Carry your affirmations with you on three-by-five-inch index cards to read from time to time. As you read, visualize yourself having achieved your desires.

It is basically that simple. To assure that you get the most from your affirmations, you may want to consider the following points:

1. Only thoughts with intense feeling bring results. You will want to repeat your affirmations until you can feel the intense desire moving you.
2. Repeat your affirmations in private. Our affirmations are our secret. We want to prove this process to ourselves, and distraction energies dilute our focus and intention.
3. Choose a time that's right for you. For many people, the best time of the day for writing or reading affirmations is upon rising in the morning and just before sleeping. Another effective time for repeating affirmations is while doing anything in a rote manner, such as long-distance highway driving. Whenever we are in a relaxed state, we have greater access to our subconscious.

In a receptive, passive mood, our brain waves dip frequently into the slower alpha wave, or meditative pattern. At these times we are more open to suggestions on the deeper levels of consciousness.

The state of mind with which we approach every step of concentrated mind action is very important. It is especially so in the visualizing and affirming steps. These two steps work well only when we are in a positive, expectant, trusting mood. At such times we feel full, connected to our source, and our personal power is at our command.

Negative states tend to destroy any good we try to start. Feelings of anger, resentment, fear, doubt, and boredom interfere with our positive programming. It seems best at these times to deliberately focus on the negative problem, to define it and to deal with it to the best of your ability. Define who did what to whom; what needs to happen that hasn't been done; and what you can do about the situation. Always look for the message in the negative: What is there for you to learn in this situation?

When you have done all you can do about a negative situation, it is time to release it. One characteristic of winners is that they know when and how to release a problem. Your subconscious will then be free to continue to work on it and later produce the perfect solution. The quickest way to release it is to return the focus of your attention to lifting your spirits. You can do this with breathing deeply, exercise, taking time to read inspiring words — whatever works to get your energies flowing in a positive way.

Pay attention to all negative thoughts that are contradicting specific affirmations. These are important messages, for they point out our blocks — ways we are keeping ourselves back. Write them down and look for themes behind the objections. For example, if you now weigh 180 pounds and your goal is 120 pounds, you may start affirming:

Affirmation	Objections
I now weigh 120 pounds.	Oh yeah! With all that junk you eat. Your lucky that you don't weigh 220 pounds.
I now weigh 120 pounds.	Not by nibbling those candy goodies all the time!
I now weigh 120 pounds.	You can't resist free food and you have a lot of social luncheons to attend.

In light of these negatives, you may want to modify your affirmations to be more realistic. Your negative statements may be telling you that you are not ready for your ideal desire yet. You may want to adjust your goals to bring change in incremental steps. For example, if you find it easier to accept your ability to be 150 pounds, start by affirming "I now weigh 150 pounds."

Affirmation and visualization are part of the natural process of manifestation that we have been using unconsciously. To develop skill at using them consciously will require dedication, commitment, and patience. Never push; there is time. Pushing doesn't work anyway. What we are learning to do is to relax into beneficial change the natural way. We all want everything yesterday, but the universe has its own time schedule. We didn't get into our present situation overnight. By knowing that our good fortune is coming, it is easier to develop patience.

The most effective affirmations are those you create for yourself, based specifically on your goals. Here are a few that clients of mine have found helpful:

Nothing has meaning except the meaning I give it.
All I have is now and now is enough.
I like being alone; my privacy is important.
I accept myself in all ways.
I approve of myself.
I welcome challenges.
I am responsible for my good health.
I have all the time I need.
I love to give and receive.
I deserve all the good that is coming to me.
My wealth is in my mind.
I now forgive everyone for every offense.
I bless my money. Each dollar I spend or give is returned multiplied.
I am always in the right place at the right time.
No is a complete sentence.
The meaning of any experience is the frame I put around it.
Complaining confirms my victim status.
The more positive thoughts I have, the more positive my life is.
I am rich; I am free.

ACTING "AS IF"

When we affirm and visualize, we are working with energies that bypass reason, forced will, and judgment of the conscious mind. We are working directly with the energy of the subconscious, which is subjective and nonjudgmental.

Effective affirmation accompanied by acts of conviction impress the subconscious. We need to actively prepare to receive by acting "as if" what we want is present. We want to act as if we are already thin, beautiful, smart, wealthy, healthy. How would you be if you had it all already?

Incorporate the law of attraction. If a trip is your goal, make out your packing list and get brochures from the travel agent. Buy that dress a size too small knowing that is what you will wear. Have your outfit planned for that job interview you want.

Some people have difficulty stating that their affirmation is already true. They feel they are lying. However, there is no incongruence here. As you visualize and affirm, your goal does already exist — in the form of an idea. Remember that nothing was ever created that did not first exist as an idea. The idea, then, is your goal in embryonic form. Therefore, you tell the truth when you affirm your desire as already happening.

By coupling affirmation and visualization with your positive action, you are insuring the full unfolding of your goal in physical reality if it is right for you. Be sure to conclude every affirmation exercise with, "This or something better, according to my divine plan."

PRACTICE RANDOM ACTS OF KINDNESS

Put your affirmations into action. Act as if what you want to have happen in your life has already happened and you are free to be a generous person — generous in all ways: let someone in line go ahead of you, smile at a clerk and speak pleasantly even when in a hurry, befriend a child or an animal, offer to help a neighbor. This helps to release the tight, self-concerned part of us which is preoccupied with "not getting" and affirms in physical reality that "I have more than enough now."

SELECTED AFFIRMATIONS

I am a beautiful, powerful woman.

I am complete, whole, and of the light.

I deserve love.

I focus on my good pure essence.

There is nothing I need to do.

I am comfortable and satisfied.

I allow myself to relax into my pure essence.

I now allow the positive in and everything is positive.

I will always find the perfect path.

I am a child of God and wish only to do his bidding.

My body is my temple within which I carry out God's will.

I am in perfect health in mind, body, and spirit.

I will always remain young and beautiful.

I am getting better and better every day in every way.

I am developing perfect eyesight.

I only desire and eat pure, good, wholesome food.

I eat only fresh fruit, fresh vegetables, yogurt, nuts, and cereals.

I exercise every day with yoga, jogging, and other aerobic
    activities.

I am learning to love myself more every day.

I am proud of myself in the presence of others.

I am more and more lovable.

I am more and more pleasing to myself every day.

I like myself as a woman.

I practice being good to myself.

I meditate twice each day.
I think only positive thoughts of others.
I dedicate my life to expressing love.
I live a life of abundance.
I feel great sexual pleasure.
I am loved greatly.
I have a beautiful, perfectly shaped body.
I have true self-confidence in all aspects of life.

18

LOVE YOUR WAY
TO PROSPERITY

"Peace of mind comes from not wanting to change others."
— Gerald Jampolsky

**PROSPERITY LAW NO. 9:
THE LAW OF LOVING**

*Whatever goodness we want for ourselves
we must also desire for others.*

If we are to prosper individually, we must see ourselves in community contributing to others — caring for, supporting, and encouraging. True prosperity comes from responsible, "right" relationships with others.

Religious doctrine and metaphysical teaching have told us that it never works to attack, make others wrong, or win at another's expense. Many don't explain why. We are taught to turn the other cheek when offended; an action based on self-sacrifice and an altruistic concern for others. We need to understand, however, that "right living" is self-serving. When we understand how we benefit, we may be motivated to move even more rapidly and effortlessly toward the ideal behavior.

The prosperity law of loving is really a statement about who we are within a context: we are each part of a delicately woven whole. Just as every living cell in our body is a self-contained, self-satisfying world, yet interdependent upon many others, so we too are autonomous, self-willed, creative beings — yet one within a whole.

We all want to win at the game of life. The emerging truth is that the best way to do this is for us to love and promote the best in each other — not for self-sacrificing reasons, but for the most powerfully motivating factor on earth: self-interest. When we catch on and play the game consciously, we all win.

The importance of this law is seen and felt in our global relations with one another. It is easy to feel helpless and defeated in the face of world problems — yet the same laws of prosperity apply as much to a culture as they do to the individual. What we do individually is a microcosm of what we do as a society. Our individual thoughts act in synergy to form a mass consensus — a subconscious idea that we reproduce in physical reality. Since our cultural consensus is a reflection of our individual thoughts and actions, we need to look inwardly at the direction of our thoughts. Globally, it is obvious that what we need is drastic revision in the way we are all using mind action.

Almost every situation in today's world is forcing us to seek a solution of balance. The problems of ecology and pollution are good examples. We are all on planet earth together — there is no escape. So our only choice is playing the game of life from either a win-win or lose-lose position.

The time is over for thinking that our problems would be solved if only one group or one thing ceases to be a threat. The consumer is the producer when it comes to environmental issues. The lines between capital and labor blur as each person learns he or she must cooperate to avoid economic collapse when faced with the threat of depression. We see the broader view of our problems if we begin to ask how we can continue to produce without polluting the environment. How can we defend without obliterating that which we already have?

How do we face these and other social issues, utilizing mind action to prosper as an individual, as a nation, and as a world?

We can start with our own individual thought, for that is where the movement of all mass thought starts.

Our mass consensus is created out of our individual consciousness. Each of us does make a difference.

This has not always been obvious. The pragmatists among us saw no ultimate social value in the personal growth movement of the 1960s and 1970s. Efforts to increase individual consciousness through awareness of body and feeling states was seen as "contemplating one's navel" — useless self-indulgence. Critics of this movement feared excessive attention on self would destroy concern for others and inhibit the work of the world. They argued that if we drew attention away from the problems of society in favor of increasing attention to self-awareness of inner wants and needs, we would become a nation of self-righteous hedonists. They pointed with alarm at boastful, self-centered personalities as prime examples of what happens with so-called "self-love" taken to the extreme.

The attitudes of these critics demonstrate the pitfalls of either/or thinking. We are creatures who need to pay attention to both our inner and outer worlds. Egotistical attitudes are not the result of increased self-love and self-confidence, but demonstrate the lack of any real self-esteem. When we feel good about ourselves there is no need to boast and bluster.

Our inner work supports our outer work. We must go inside to contact our higher self for regeneration, self-approval, and self-direction. For that knowledge to be of real value, however, we must express it in the world as creative, loving action helping humankind.

Far from being useless, spending time, money, and energy on one's own self-awareness is the only firm foundation for ultimate solutions to world problems. Guns and bombs create temporary "solutions" which lead to ever bigger problems. Becoming self-aware is a process of changing attitudes — of becoming more fully human.

The more fully human we are, the more we can understand the condition of our oneness. The more we see through the peripheral actions to the essence of each other, the more loving we can be. We come to realize that no one has ever done anything that we haven't at least thought of at one time in our life. We therefore learn to forgive — the highest human faculty we have.

Exploitive action comes from the mass thought that there is not enough — love, money, sex, energy, power, land, water, food, time, health, opportunity. Yet there is no shortage of any of these. We have plenty of everything we need to be happy. The only barriers to abundance are our beliefs about the inevitability of scarcity.

Ask yourself what beliefs you hold about scarcity in your life. Make a list of everything that is truly important for a good life. Almost everyone feels there is not enough time; yet there are still twenty-four hours each day — the same as always. Shortage of time always indicates a need to reprioritize.

Many yearn for love and feel there is not enough of it in the world. I've heard many women and men express the feeling that there aren't many good people around to choose from. There are plenty of wonderful people — both men and women — wanting to give and receive love. Love already exists inside us. We limit ourselves only because of our shields of fear, our shields against feeling vulnerable.

We hear so much about the energy crisis. The only crisis we are facing is the challenge to create new forms of energy to use as our fossil fuel is burning up. All that exists in the universe is energy. There is no lack of energy, only lack of commitment to find new sources.

Water itself is not scarce. Clean water is scarce. How we decide to use the bountiful supply of water we have is what determines its purity. Those decisions are dependent upon our consciousness.

Then there's money. We own the bank that supplies our wealth. It is the natural flow of our creative energy that overflows into money. When we are living a loving, giving life, fully conscious of who we are and what we want, we have the ability to obtain all the money we need through our creative ideas.

Our universe isn't skimpy. We are oversupplied in great abundance — with love.

Coming from a new consciousness of abundance, we can see that winning is an attitude and happiness is a decision. We can release and relax into our prosperity when we know, affirm, visualize, and experience the love of the universe through the abundance that surrounds us. By expressing love for each other and the earth, we are only paying back a little of that which we have already received.

19

PROSPERITY TUNE-UP

"As a being of power, intelligence, and love, and the lord of your own thoughts, you contain within yourself that transforming and regenerative agency by which you may make yourself what you will."

— James Allen

Now that you've read this far and done the work, you are ready to reap your rewards. I'm sure your life has already been changing in many ways as you have incorporated the prosperity keys and laws into your life. To promote your prosperity even more, you may want to review the following Prosperity Consciousness Tune-up Checklist from time to time, asking yourself the following questions and contemplating the answers you receive. This process may help you get in touch with ways you are still holding back from your full prosperity.

Keep in your consciousness the idea that only thought stands between you and what you desire. By changing your consciousness, you change your world. Where your mind goes, creative energy flows.

PROSPERITY CONSCIOUSNESS TUNE-UP CHECKIST

1. How well do I know myself and what I want? Until we know who we are, we can't know what we want.

2. Do I really want to succeed? How much? We only get what we want deep down.

3. Have I developed a strong power of concentration — an ability to focus on one thing at a time? Scattered desires create scattered results.

4. Do I basically feel that I have choice in life? To take responsibility is to recognize choice in attitude.

5. Do I feel life is pretty much okay the way it is? We have to start from where we are — that means accepting what is first.

6. Do I know my basic purpose in life? Once we know the answer to this, it's much easier to know the answers to our other questions.

7. Am I willing to take calculated risks to get what I want? We'll never know enough. At one point, we have to be willing to jump into the unknown armed only with our intuitive feelings.

8. How can I feel more comfortable spending, receiving, saving, and investing money? Money is our helpful ally.

9. Do I feel like a complete, whole person even if I happen to be temporarily without money or a partner in my life?

10. Given my talents, do I know what the universe expects from me? What does the world need that can best be done by me?

11. Have I cleared a space for success in my life? Some people are still giving energy to things that happened five, ten, fifteen years ago. We need to release situations, people, and things to make room for the new.

12. Have I forgiven everyone I need to forgive? Holding resentments takes both hands. To reach out for the love, joy, and success in all ways of life, we want to free ourselves of the burden of resentment — not for the sake of others, but for ourselves!

13. Have I reconciled my conflicting desires? Is one part of me holding back what another part wants? Am I listening to both sides? Remember that the power of suppressed desires sabotages those desires we're going after.

14. Am I specific in my direction? Every good ship's captain knows her course before taking her ship to sea. You will only know when you get there if you know where you're going.

15. Am I thinking big enough? Have you given yourself enough challenge in your goal? Sometimes we don't get our goal because something much greater than we dreamed possible is in store for us.

16. Am I willing to change my direction if it seems appropriate? Am I flexible enough to shift gears if I see that I need to? It is difficult to get started toward a goal if we have little faith in our brake and steering mechanisms. No goal is absolute or forever. Give yourself the right to say no to a goal, to change your mind freely and to feel good about your ability to stay flexible.

17. Would my achieving this goal be good for everyone concerned? Unloving goals are not prospering goals. Is it right for me to have it? Does it really belong to me? We need to know our intentions behind our goals.

18. Does this goal fit my personality, physical strength, psychological makeup, and values? Sometimes an intuitive knowingness cancels our order if it is inconsistent with our basic self. Does this goal fit you?

19. Do I really want what I'm pursuing? Our desires change, but sometimes we've forgotten to update our goals to keep pace. Have you ever wondered why buying something you wanted last year doesn't make you happy now? We need to check our goal list periodically. Maybe we're not getting a certain goal because we no longer want it!

20. Can I name a salary that I feel I'm worthy of? How much are you willing to give yourself?

21. Can I eliminate each negative thought as it comes into my mind? This is the most important act of all.

22. Have I released feelings of hurry, worry, and doubt about my progress toward prosperity? One of the main themes of this book is that prosperity thoughts produce prosperous situations. We

cannot be hurrying, worrying, and doubting and still be producing true prosperity. We want to do what we can do: choose our goal well; meditate on it; visualize it; affirm it; and allow the experience of having achieved it to fill us. Then we can go about our lives in peace, knowing it is coming. We must allow for divine timing. Many give up too soon. Be patient. Not a single blossom flowers before its time.

23. Am I listening to feedback on my venture? We want to achieve prosperity, not bloody our heads against a solid wall. If you are not being successful, if doors are not opening, pay attention to the signs. This may not be the way for you to go. Forcing creates the opposite effect of what you want. Persistence and patience pay, but when you are on the right path, you know it, you feel it along the way. If you are still finding yourself in situations that make you feel miserable, know that pain is caused by holding on to negative thought. Is there something you need to release? Are there other paths, not explored yet, that may be better suited for your purposes? Negative feedback is an invaluable part of finding the perfect solution. It may be time to check out other possibilities.

24. Am I letting go of being timid? Am I being assertive in situations that call for it? Loving by itself is not enough in this world. We have the right and duty to protect ourselves. Action based on love, combined with wisdom, gives us all the strength we need to stand up for ourselves, and to give to others without being "used."

25. Am I unattached to the end result? If it would upset you not to achieve prosperity immediately, you will probably benefit by letting go and letting up on yourself. Attachments act as blocks to getting our "good." The upset is caused by fear of "not getting." We energize this fear with our attachment, thereby creating that which we fear.

26. Do I believe that I deserve and will achieve success in life? We only achieve and maintain what we believe we deserve.

SUMMARY:
YOU CAN HAVE IT
IF YOU REALLY WANT IT!

*"Those who cherish a beautiful vision, a lofty ideal
in their hearts, will one day realize it."*

— James Allen

Writing this book has been an exciting adventure for me, and a concrete example of manifestation. When I first wrote this book I had taken a year's leave of absence from college teaching to write, visualizing and affirming from the start this book's existence in print.

The physical setting in which I had chosen to write it was also a culmination of a ten-year-old dream. With my new husband Jerry, I had moved onto a houseboat in the San Francisco Bay, where most of my twelve-hour composing and typing days were spent out on the deck, enjoying the beautiful surroundings. All of this came about through visualization, affirmation, and meditation.

Every chapter was a new confrontation with myself, as I found I could write about nothing I had left undone in my own life. Just as in teaching, I could write only about what I was living. Although little of what I have written is original in concept, it is so thoroughly integrated into my life that these ideas are no longer a technique outside myself; they were and are now a way of life. It has been an act of love to review sources and filter information through my own experience, to put it all together in an understandable form, so that we may communicate together.

Prosperity consciousness is not something you just get and then have the rest of your life. Once you get it, you never lose it, but we all need to be reminded of it at times. As one of my favorite teachers told me, "I'm teaching you so there will be more of us out there living it — then you can remind me when I forget."

I encourage you to create your daily routine today that supports living the life you fantasize for tomorrow. Here is a routine I've found helpful:

MORNING ROUTINE
Visualizing and Affirming Process

1. Read goals:
    - Of the year, once a month.
    - Of the month, once a week.
    - Of the week, every day.
    - Choose one goal for today to focus on.

2. Visualize goals:
    - From your visualization notebook.
    - Concentrate on the chosen goal for the day.

3. Affirm weekly affirmations:
    - Repeat affirmations out loud five times.
    - Concentrate on the chosen goal for the day.

4. Write your affirmation of the day ten times.

5. Eyes closed process:
    - Breathe deeply three times, close eyes, and relax.

- See the word RELAX on the inside of your forehead.
- Let your whole body "melt" into the floor or chair as you let go even more.
- With each exhalation, count down from ten to one and repeat the word "deeper."
- When totally relaxed, nonverbally:

  Affirm your oneness with universal energy.

  Thank Infinite Intelligence for all you already have.

  Forgive all who have offended you; include yourself.

  Declare the negative attitude you are prepared to give up today.

  Affirm your goals of the week "as if" they have already happened.
- Visualize your goals of the week "as if" they are already yours.
- Feel now how you will feel when your goals are manifested.
- Finish with "This or something better, with good for all concerned."
- Allow your mind to become still and quiet — remain in concentrated quiet listening.
- Count from one to ten, repeating, "Every day in every way I am feeling better and better," with each breath.
- Open your eyes, feeling alive, awake, enthusiastic, ready to do the work that only you can do to manifest your dreams, feeling assured of success.

Keep your visualization notebook with your yearly, monthly, and weekly goal sheets all together where you do your daily inner work.

This whole process is based on the following five key thoughts that you may want to remind yourself of:

1. By daily thanking the universe for the love and good that you already have in your life, you are acknowledging your oneness with universal energy, and the wheels are set in motion to manifest your desires.

2. By concentrating on choosing wisely what you want, not only are you going to be satisfied, but you are willing to realize the consequences and are ready to pay the price for what you want.

3. When you can relax with a quiet mind, you have access to another reality of the higher self. This inner communication is your real work of life. Your outer work is but a reflection of this inner work.

4. Meditation is the means of consulting with the higher self who is available at all times, and knowledgeable on all issues concerning you. When you stay in meditation long enough to:
   a. Ask for direction
   b. Visualize your desires
   c. Affirm with feeling that the goals are yours
   d. Listen with focused awareness
   you receive the insights guiding you to your next step.

5. Your ability to give and to forgive are the gifts from Infinite Intelligence which allow you to open up receptively to the bounty of the universe.

EVENING ROUTINE

An evening routine is equally important. Ten minutes before falling asleep:

1. Review your day.
   Are there incidents you need to "repair"? If so, visualize yourself going through that incident, handling it just the way you wish you had done it. Then release it.

2. Review your most important goal.
   Give instruction to your inside awareness to bring this goal into being with good for all concerned.

3. Ask for dreams with clear messages.
   Keep your dream journal handy to record important feeling

dreams with messages about your life situations.
4.   Give thanks to the universe for a good night's restful sleep.

Fortunately, we will never unravel the infinite mysteries of life, so there will be no end to the fun of trying to. With these exercises, routines, and new ways of thinking, we are leaning to chart our course, going with the tide of universal energy, guaranteed to take us to whatever is best for us. The energy focused by the subconscious manifests in so many ways, with no barriers in time or space to stop it, that we must always be prepared for the unexpected ways our dreams are realized.

Once you have awakened to your true nature, your real purpose, and have an appreciation of all the opportunities of abundance around you, you have also awakened your power to create more than you need of everything in your life. Now that you know you will succeed because you have the tools to assure that success, you are ready to expect everything and know that *you already have it all*. Enjoy!

KEYS TO PROSPERITY

Prosperity Key No. 1:
   We reap what we sow.   Chapter 4

Prosperity Key No. 2:
   Proving ourselves right has its consequences.   Chapter 4

Prosperity Key No. 3:
   To receive more, we must be willing to give more.   Chapter 5

Prosperity Key No. 4:
   Our personal power formula is: $E=MC^2$.   Chapter 6

Prosperity Key No. 5:
   We are all we need because we are what we desire.   Chapter 7

Prosperity Key No. 6:
   Love yourself first.   Chapter 7

Prosperity Key No. 7:
   Quieting the mind promotes directed action.   Chapter 8

Prosperity Key No. 8:
   Forgive all who have offended you —
   not for them, but for yourself.   Chapter 13

Prosperity Key No. 9:
   Spend your money with the consciousness of
   giving with love.   Chapter 13

PROSPERITY LAWS

Prosperity Law No. 1: The Law of Self-Awareness   Chapter 10
*We can only have what we want when we know who we
are and what we want.*

Prosperity Law No. 2: The Law of Wanting   Chapter 11
*Experiencing choice means knowing what we want and
why we want it. Only then do we have the excitement
and energy to go after our desires.*

Prosperity Law No. 3: The Law of Planning   Chapter 12
Without planning there is no consistent prosperity.

Prosperity Law No. 4: The Law of Releasing   Chapter 13
*We must get rid of what we don't want to make room
for what we do.*

Prosperity Law No. 5: The Law of Compensation   Chapter 14
There is a price for everything and we always pay.

Prosperity Law No. 6: The Law of Attraction   Chapter 15
We attract what we are.

Prosperity Law No. 7: The Law of Visualization   Chapter 16
We become what we imagine, positive or negative.

Prosperity Law No. 8: The Law of Affirmation   Chapter 17
*We become what we want to be by affirming and acting
on our belief that we already are there.*

Prosperity Law No. 9: The Law of Loving   Chapter 18
*Whatever goodness we want for ourselves we must
also desire for others.*

BIBLIOGRAPHY

Here are a few of the books and publications that Ruth found helpful in her first edition of *Prospering Woman*. She listed them in five categories: mental, physical, emotional, spiritual, and financial prosperity. There has been an explosion of materials since this first bibliography came out, but Ruth was not able to rewrite this section of her book before she died. Following this original bibliography, we have included some of the books she recommended to her family and friends at various times, and books that we found in her library.

Mental prosperity is the foundation of all other prosperity. It is opening our minds to the wisdom of cosmic consciousness. It is allowing the transformation that takes place once we realize who we are and our role in the universe as conscious creatures. When we know who we are, it follows naturally that we are able to receive what we want.

The Roots of Consciousness rev. ed. by Jeffrey Mishlove. Country Oaks Books, 1992. A provocative, comprehensive study of consciousness and the powers of the mind. This is a well-documented, scholarly approach to consciousness.

The Aquarian Conspiracy, Personal & Social Transformation in Our Time rev. ed. by Marilyn Ferguson. J.P. Tarcher, Inc., Los Angeles, CA, 1987. Invaluable reference book for understanding what's happening in the transformation of human consciousness.

The Metaphoric Mind rev. and updated ed. by Bob Samples. Jalmar Press, Torrance, CA, 1993.

Exploring the Crack in the Metaphoric Mind by Joseph Chilton Pearce. Pocket Books, New York, NY, 1974.

Experiences in Visual Thinking 2nd ed. by Robert McKim. P.W.S. Publishing, Boston, MA, 1980. A book designed to help you be a more flexible, productive thinker utilizing the subconscious as well as the conscious mind.

The Experience of Insight by Joseph Goldstein. Shambhala Publications, Boston, MA, 1987.

The Natural Mind rev. ed. by Andrew Weil. Houghton-Mifflin, Boston, MA, 1986.

Mind as Healer, Mind as Slayer by Kenneth R. Pelletier. Dell Publishing, New York, NY, 1977. Recommended for understanding the relationship of human consciousness to stress.

The Science of Mind by Ernest Holmes. Putnam Berkeley Group, New York, NY, 1989. Prophet for the new age by his early recognition of mind action in creating physical reality.

The Path of Action by Jack Schwarz. NAL-Dutton, New York, NY, 1977. He writes of the creative source within you — the spirit that flows through you — the source of prosperity.

The Master Game by Robert De Ropp. Dell Publishing, New York, NY, 1989. A demystified version of Oespensky. This is a great book for looking at purpose in life. The master game, of course, is self-awareness.

The Lazy Man's Guide to Enlightenment by Thaddeus Golas. Bantam Books, New York, NY, 1983.

Sixty Seconds to Mind Expansion by Harold Cook and Joel Davitz. Pocket Books, New York, NY, 1976.

Acres of Diamonds by Russell H. Conwell. Tree of Life Publications, Joshua Tree, CA, 1993. A classic among prosperity thinkers. Your golden opportunity is wherever you are.

Open Your Mind to Prosperity rev. ed. by Catherine Ponder. DeVorss & Co., Marina Del Rey, CA, 1984. Simply written, religious descriptions of the process of getting what you want in life through love and right living.

Brain Mind Bulletin, 4717 N. Figueroa St., Los Angeles, CA 90042. A two-page monthly bulletin. Has information on the latest scientific research and breakthroughs on understanding conscious evolution and the role of consciousness as an energy force.

Paths to Power by Natasha Josephowitz, Ph.D. Addison-Wesley, Redding, MA, 1990.

Physical prosperity is creating the healthy, vibrant, beautiful body we all want. There is no one standard for what this means. Only you determine what you want from your physical body. Here are some books to help you achieve it.

The Pritikin Program for Diet and Exercise by Nathan Pritikin and Patricia McGrady. Bantam Books, New York, NY, 1984. I personally agree with Pritikin's ideas on cutting way down on sugar, white flour, fat, and salt. It's made a big difference in my health. This book has excellent recipes which means you can have a healthy diet that tastes good too.

Awareness Through Movement by Moshe Feldenkrais. Harper San Francisco, San Francisco, CA, 1991.

The Massage Book by George Downing. Bookworks Pubs., Palm Desert, CA, 1972. Prosperity is exchanging a wonderful massage with a loving friend.

New Bodies, Ourselves rev. and expanded, by The Boston Women's Health Book Collective. Simon & Schuster, New York, NY, 1992.

The Healing Mind: You Can Cure Yourself Without Drugs by Irving Oyle. Celestial Arts, Berkeley, CA, 1974.

For Yourself, Fulfillment of Female Sexuality by Lonnie Garfield Barbach. NAL-Dutton, New York, NY, 1976.

Are You Confused? by Paavo Airola, Ph.D. Health Plus, Phoenix, AZ, 1982. Physical prosperity demands that we become aware of and follow a nutritious food plan.

The Relaxation Response by Herbert Benson, M.D. and Miriam Z. Klipper. Avon, New York, NY, 1976. An excellent resource for understanding the physical benefits of relaxation.

The Relaxation & Stress Reduction Workbook rev. ed. by Martha Davis Ph.D and Elizabeth Robbins Eshelman. New Harbinger Publications, Oakland, CA, 1988.

Emotional prosperity happens when we align our feelings with our mental, physical, spiritual, and financial goals, and achieve them. As we know our purpose in life, expand our ability to love, become able to say yes and no and feel good about ourselves in the process, experience a positive attitude toward ourselves and others, and feel comfortable with our independence, we are developing our emotional prosperity.

These are a few of the books offering clarity on how to become more emotionally prosperous.

How to Be Your Own Best Friend by Mildred Newman and Bernard Berkowitz. Ballentine, New York, NY, 1986.

The Angry Book by Theodore Rubin, M.D. Macmillan Publishing, Indianapolis, IN, 1993.

Love by Leo Buscaglia. Fawcett, New York, NY, 1993. To prosper is to love, and to love is to prosper.

Women as Winners by Dorothy Jongeward and Dru Scott. Addison-Wesley Publishing Co., Redding, MA, 1976.

The Dynamic Laws of Prosperity rev. ed. by Catherine Ponder. DeVorss & Co., Marina Del Rey, CA, 1985. Her books are devoted to understanding the prospering messages of the Bible.

Love is Letting Go of Fear by Gerald G. Jampolsky, M.D. Celestial Arts, Berkeley, CA, 1995. Based on the Course in Miracles, this little book can go with you anywhere and provide the stimulus for hours of contemplation on what emotional prosperity is all about.

Pulling Your Own Strings by Dr. Wayne Dyer. Avon, New York, NY, 1979.

Intimacy, the Essence of Male and Female by Shirley Luthman. Ivy Books, New York, NY, 1990.

The Magical Child Within You by Bruce Davis, Ph.D. and Genny Wright. Celestial Arts, Berkeley, CA, 1985. Prosperity is the result of our creative ideas — the playground of our child within.

The Transparent Self by Sidney Jourard. Van Nostrand Reinhold, New York, NY, 1971.

Power From Within by Marguerite Craig, et al. ProActive Press, Berkeley, CA, 1977.

Ability to Love by Allan Fromme. Wilshire Book Co., No. Hollywood, CA, 1977. A book that was personally important to me in discovering the process we all go through in learning to love. Helps to explain why some relationships aren't working.

Spiritual prosperity can be stated the simplest of all — it is finding our oneness with all there is. When we experience unity we then realize that that which we desire is not separate from us. I recommend these books for further understanding of this principle.

Emerson's Essays, Ralph Waldo Emerson, intro. by Irwin Edman. HarperCollins Publishers, 1981. Emerson is not only one of the greatest thinkers, he's one of the most outstanding prosperity thinkers we have ever produced. Reading him you feel renewed, inspired, and begin to believe in yourself as a naturally prospering being.

Selected Writings of Ralph Waldo Emerson, Ralph W. Emerson, ed. by Brooks Atkinson, Random House, New York, NY, 1977.

You Are the World by J. Krishnamurti. HarperCollins Publishers, New York, NY, 1989. The message is in the title. Penetrating discussion on the role of thought in creating reality. He will definitely make you think.

The Tao of Physics 3rd rev. and updated ed. by Fritjof Capra. Shambhala Publications, Boston, MA, 1991. Quantum physics is proving we are all part of the same whole.

How to Meditate by Lawrence LeShan. Bantam Books, New York, NY, 1984. Meditation is one of the most powerful tools we can use for achieving prosperity.

Phenomenon of Man by Teilhard De Chardin. HarperCollins, New York, NY, 1975. Evolution is first and foremost, he says, the evolution of the psychic. A "nomad of science" in search of the secret of our rightful place in the scheme of nature. He concluded that all matter is developing toward the phenomenon of consciousness — the only reason for existence.

Prosperity by Charles Fillmore. Unity Books, Missouri, 1936.

Financial prosperity is having the means — money and other resources — to carry out our dreams. Financial prosperity is an integral part of our fulfilled nature, and is a natural result of having pursued our mental, physical, emotional, and spiritual prosperity. Here are some excellent books to develop your consciousness of money and financial planning.

Complete Estate Planning Guide rev. ed. by Robert Brosterman and Kathleen Adams. NAL-Dutton, New York, NY, 1994.

The Only Investment Guide You'll Ever Need rev. ed. by Andrew Tobias. Bantam Books, New York, NY, 1983.

Think & Grow Rich by Napoleon Hill. Napoleon Hill Foundation, Northbrook, IL, 1989.

The Greatest Secret in the World by Og Mandino. Bantam Books, New York, NY, 1983.

Money Love by Jerry Gillies. Warner Publishing, New York, NY, 1981.

**ALSO READ: MONEY MAGAZINE, CHANGING TIMES,
AND WALL STREET JOURNAL.**

Techniques for visualizing:

Creative Visualization rev. and updated by Shakti Gawain. New World Library, San Rafael, CA, 1995. If I could only take one book away with me to a desert island I would take this book. Well written with deep insight, Shakti tells us how everyone can visualize — easily, and thereby create their own prosperity.

Seeing with the Mind's Eye, the History, Techniques and Uses of Visualization by Mike Samuels, M.D. and Nancy Samuels. Random House, New York, NY, 1975. An adventure story of exploring the inner world through visualization. Shows how mental images influence people's lives, and how by holding positive images lives are transformed positively.

Health, Youth and Beauty Through Color Breathing by Linda Clark and Yvonne Martine. Celestial Arts, Berkeley, CA, 1976. Aging is an attitude. We can choose to stay young-looking and -feeling. This book describes a wonderful technique for visualizing breath in different colors to facilitate a more youthful appearance.

The Zen of Seeing by Frederick Franck. Vintage Books, Random House, New York, NY, 1973. A delightful book on seeing and drawing as meditation. It requires stopping our preoccupations long enough to look at life. Enjoying the moment is a prosperity feeling always available. Our ability to visualize internally is greatly enhanced by our ability to "see" physically.

Techniques for affirming:

I Deserve Love by Sondra Ray. Celestial Arts, Berkeley, CA, 1987. Outlines in detail how to use affirmation, or autosuggestion for personal fulfillment.

Techniques for working through conflict between goals:

Psychosynthesis by Roberto Assagioli. Viking Penguin, New York, NY, 1971.

Techniques for making a career choice:

What Color is Your Parachute? by Richard Bolles. Ten Speed Press, Berkeley, CA, 1972.

If You Don't Know Where You Are Going, You'll Probably End Up Somewhere Else by David P. Campbell. Tabor Pub, Allen, TX, 1990.

Work with Passion rev. and updated by Nancy Anderson. New World Library, San Rafael, CA, 1995.

Techniques for working with the subconscious mind:

Silva Mind Control Method by Jose Silva. Pocket Books, New York, NY, 1991.

Living Your Dreams by Gayle Delaney. HarperCollins, New York, NY, 1988.

Techniques for releasing negative thinking:

Handbook to Higher Consciousness 5th ed. by Ken Keyes, Jr. Love Line Books, Coos Bay, OR, 1975. If you know where you want to go, but you feel stuck in where you are, this may be the book for you. Designed to show you how to use your mind creatively — how to release self-defeating attitudes and habits of thought.

Note from Kathy (Ross) Hartwig: Here are some of the books Ruth recommended to me before she died, and that I feel would be excellent sources for readers:

The Misunderstood Child 2nd ed. by Larry Silver. McGraw-Hill, New York, NY, 1991. An excellent book for parents who have children with suspected ADD. We have found it invaluable in helping our family circle.

Men are From Mars, Women are From Venus by John Gray, Ph.D. HarperCollins, New York, NY, 1992. A wonderful source for looking at the many different ways of loving and appreciating our partners.

Bradshaw on: The Family by John Bradshaw. Health Communications, Inc., Deerfield Beach, FL, 1988. A good book about the many addictions and dysfunctional family problems we all face.

How to Survive the Loss of a Love by Melba Colgrove, et al. Prelude Press, Los Angeles, CA, 1993. This book was given to me after Mom's sudden, unexpected death, and helped me through some very difficult times. I highly recommend this book to anyone suffering in one way or another the ending of a relationship.

A Vegetarian's Ecstasy by J. Levin M.D. and N. Cederquist. GLO, INC., San Diego, CA, 1994. On a different note, this was the last book Mom gave me, and it is exciting! So many great recipes and low fat, low sodium, good tasting meals, everyone should try these, vegetarians or not.

The McDougall Program: Twelve Days to Dynamic Health by John McDougall M.D. NAL-Dutton, New York, NY, 1990. Our whole family has benefitted from this wonderful guide to lowering blood pressure and in general being healthy through eating the right foods. Great recipes, too.

Books recommended by Becky (Ross) Davis — given to her by Ruth Ross:

Seven Steps to Inner Power by Tae Yun Kim, New World Library, San Rafael, CA, 1991.

Codependent No More by Melody Beattie. Harper San Francisco, 1987.

Language of Letting Go by Melody Beattie. HarperCollins, New York, NY, 1990.

The Seven Habits of Highly Effective People by Steven Covey. Fireside, New York, NY, 1989.

When Money is the Drug by Donna Boundy. Harper San Francisco, 1994.

The Enneagram by Helen Palmer. Harper San Francisco, 1988.

Women Who Love Too Much by Robin Norwood. Pocket Books, Simon & Schuster, 1985.

ABOUT THE AUTHOR

*R*uth Ross, Ph.D., was the daughter of a tenant farmer. She was born in 1929, and lived a childhood life of poverty. She decided at an early age that she would never be poor again.

Ruth married Frank Ross in 1948, and had two daughters, Kathy and Becky. She returned to college after her daughters were in school, developed a successful career in counseling, and completed a doctorate degree in family counseling. She was divorced, and married Jerry Haas in 1978. Along the way, she achieved her goals of independence and a deep awareness of the many facets of prosperity, and realized how to achieve them.

Ruth was a spiritual person, an ardent supporter of women's interests, and a creator of self-awareness seminars that created an atmosphere of trust, joy, and excitement. Her seminars on prosperity emphasized that "attaining what we desire for our financial, physical, and mental well-being is not only possible, it is a necessary part of the balance in being human. Abundance is a natural state of being."

On January 20, 1994, after a full day with friends, Ruth suffered a brain hemorrhage, and died peacefully on January 21. With love and devotion we have compiled all the notes, additions, and new interviews that Ruth wanted to share with you to make your life full and abundant. We would like to hear your reactions to your experiences of your own "magical happenings" when you apply these timeless, universal prosperity principles to your life. You may write us in care of New World Library.

Lovingly,

Kathy (Ross) Hartwig
Becky (Ross) Davis
Jerry Haas

RECOMMENDED READING

NEW WORLD LIBRARY is dedicated to publishing books and cassettes that help improve the quality of our lives. If you enjoyed *Prospering Woman*, we highly recommend the following books:

Work with Passion by Nancy Anderson. This step-by-step program follows the ten "Passion Secrets" of powerful people. A comprehensive course in career counseling that awakens the joys of working at what we love the most.

Creating Affluence by Deepak Chopra. Outlines simple steps and everyday actions that create wealth effortlessly and joyfully. A lifelong companion, destined to be read and referred to again and again.

The Seven Spiritual Laws of Success by Deepak Chopra. If you are not creating the life you want for yourself easily and effortlessly, you need only to look to this book and see which of these laws you may be forgetting. A powerful tool for success.

Creative Visualization by Shakti Gawain. This classic work (over two million copies sold) shows us how to use the power of our imagination to create what we want in life.

The Instant Millionaire by Mark Fisher. A tale of wisdom and wealth loaded with specific financial advice.

The Message of a Master by John McDonald. A classic tale of wealth, wisdom, and the secret of success.

If you would like a catalog of our fine
books and cassettes, contact:
NEW WORLD LIBRARY
14 PAMARON WAY
NOVATO, CA 94949
(415) 884·2100 • Fax: (415) 884-2199
Or call toll free: (800) 227·3900